Better Homes and Gardens®

ENCYCLOPEDIA
of
COOKING

Volume 15

Perk up your pickle and olive relish plate with Carrot-Olive Slaw. It's simple to make. Just combine shredded carrots and sliced, ripe olives with a vinegar-oil dressing.

On the cover: Hilo Franks and pineapple slices brown over a table-size hibachi. The apricot preserves glaze gives the sizzling meat and fruit a tempting, tart-sweet coating.

BETTER HOMES AND GARDENS BOOKS
NEW YORK • DES MOINES

© Meredith Corporation, 1970, 1971, 1973. All Rights Reserved.
Printed in the United States of America.
Special Edition. First Printing.
Library of Congress Catalog Card Number: 73-83173
SBN: 696-02035-1

PUDDING—A baked, boiled, or steamed food with a soft or spongy consistency that can be served in a variety of ways—as a main dish, side dish, or dessert. This definition of pudding applies to a vast assortment of dishes such as blood pudding, corn pudding, oyster pudding, plum pudding, tapioca pudding, and cream pudding.

None of these puddings has a staple ingredient, although flour, milk, and eggs are quite often used. Before the eleventh century, the British reportedly combined these ingredients to make puddings, and three hundred years later, flour, milk, and eggs constituted the basics for the first Yorkshire pudding, which is now famous as a traditional accompaniment for roast beef. As the culinary art was developed, other ingredients were added to puddings. During the next few centuries, puddings became more than staple dishes with the addition of fruits and liquors, as in the rich, moist plum pudding.

When the Pilgrims landed at Plymouth Rock, they returned to the simple pudding recipes. Their meager supplies and limited time for the luxury of specialized cooking led them to utilize the foods that were on hand. The hasty pudding made of flour, eggs, milk, and sometimes, oatmeal or cornmeal is a good example. So, too, is Indian pudding, a dish made of cornmeal. Later Americans added raisins or fresh fruit for a simple sweet pudding. In more recent years tapioca and cornstarch puddings have been popularly served to generations of Americans. Today, many of these old-fashioned puddings still exist in the modern homemaker's pudding list.

Types of puddings: Although at first glance the word pudding seems to apply to a diverse group of dishes that bear little or no relation to each other, a closer look reveals that puddings can be classified as either savory or sweet.

Savory puddings are used either as a main dish or as a side dish. Although the classic example of a savory pudding is the British favorite, puffy Yorkshire Pudding (see *Yorkshire Pudding* for recipe), puddings made with chicken, oysters, corn, and other meats, seafoods, or vegetables are also savory puddings. Most of these de-lectable dishes have a custardlike consistency and should be served while hot.

Carrot-Cheese Pudding

Delight the family with a new vegetable pudding—

    3 cups shredded carrots
    2 cups cooked long-grain rice
    6 ounces process American
        cheese, shredded (1½ cups)
    1 cup milk
    2 beaten eggs
    2 tablespoons instant minced onion
    1 teaspoon salt
    ¼ teaspoon pepper
            • • •
    2 ounces process American
        cheese, shredded (½ cup)

Cook carrots, covered, in 1 cup water for 10 minutes; drain. Combine with cooked long-grain rice, the 1½ cups shredded cheese, milk, eggs, instant minced onion, salt, and pepper. Turn into a 1½ quart casserole. Top with additional ½ cup shredded cheese. Bake, uncovered, at 350° for about 1 hour. Makes 6 servings.

During the last few centuries, *sweet puddings* have come into vogue. In fact, these dessert puddings are so popular that today the word pudding almost invariably conjures up visions of creamy vanilla or chocolate pudding, or lusciously warm plum pudding.

Since this type of pudding includes a great many variations, sweet puddings are further divided into steamed, baked, boiled and convenience pudding products.

(**1.**) Steamed puddings are cooked by steaming them for several hours. Since these puddings have a firm, almost cake-like texture that enables them to hold a shape well, they are often cooked in an attractive mold. Frequently, a sweet sauce is served along with steamed pudding.

(**2.**) Baked puddings, which often have a spongy or a custardlike consistency, are thickened with ingredients such as eggs, rice, or bread. This type of pudding is enjoyed by many homemakers because it doesn't require attention while it bakes.

Applesauce Pudding

8 slices firm-textured white bread
1 16-ounce can applesauce
1/3 cup raisins
1/2 teaspoon ground cinnamon
1/2 cup brown sugar
2 eggs
2 1/2 cups milk
1/2 teaspoon vanilla

Spread one side of each slice bread with butter or margarine. If desired, remove crusts. Arrange 4 slices bread, buttered side up, in greased 8x8x2-inch baking dish. Mix applesauce, raisins, cinnamon, and *2 tablespoons* of the brown sugar. Spread over bread in dish.

Cut each remaining slice bread into 4 triangles; arrange on filling, covering entire surface. Beat together eggs, milk, vanilla, 1/4 teaspoon salt, and remaining brown sugar. Pour over bread. Sprinkle with additional cinnamon. Bake at 350° for 50 to 55 minutes. Serves 6 to 8.

(3.) Probably the most popular type of pudding is boiled pudding. Creamy, cornstarch-thickened vanilla, chocolate, butterscotch, and coconut cream puddings as well as other puddings that are cooked on top of the range, such as quick-cooking tapioca pudding, belong to this group.

(4.) In recent years convenience pudding products have become very popular. These products include regular (require cooking to thicken) and instant (thicken without cooking) pudding mixes, which, when combined with milk and sometimes eggs, make a pudding similar to a cream pudding. Canned puddings which are ready-to-eat are also popular items.

Orange Tapioca Fluff

In a 1 1/2-quart saucepan combine 2 tablespoons quick-cooking tapioca, 2 tablespoons sugar, and dash salt. Blend in 1 egg yolk and 1 cup orange juice; let stand 5 minutes. Bring to boil over medium heat, stirring often. Remove from heat. Beat 1 egg white till soft peaks form; gradually add 2 tablespoons sugar, beating till stiff peaks form. Fold orange mixture into egg white; chill. Serves 2 or 3.

Vanilla Pudding

Also try chocolate and butterscotch variations—

3/4 cup sugar
2 tablespoons cornstarch
1/4 teaspoon salt
2 cups milk
   . . .
2 slightly beaten egg yolks *or*
   1 well-beaten egg
2 tablespoons butter or margarine
1 teaspoon vanilla

In saucepan blend sugar, cornstarch, and salt; add milk. Cook over medium heat, stirring constantly, till thickened and bubbly. Cook and stir 2 minutes more. Remove from heat.

Stir small amount of hot mixture into beaten egg yolks *or* well-beaten egg; return to hot mixture. Cook, stirring constantly, 2 minutes more. Remove the mixture from heat; add butter or margarine and vanilla. Pour pudding into sherbets; chill. Makes 4 or 5 servings.

Chocolate Pudding

Follow directions for Vanilla Pudding, increasing sugar to 1 cup. Add two 1-ounce squares unsweetened chocolate along with the milk.

Butterscotch Pudding

Follow directions for Vanilla Pudding, substituting brown sugar for the granulated sugar. Increase butter or margarine to 3 tablespoons.

How to use: Although pudding is commonly thought of as a dessert in itself, it can also be used as the basis for other desserts. Cream puddings particularly are adaptable to other uses, especially since the introduction of pudding mixes.

Pies constitute one of the most popular uses for puddings. For example, a cream pie is actually pudding in a pastry shell. Although simple vanilla, chocolate, or coconut cream pies are easy to make, elaborate cream pies present few problems. Just add fruit, nuts, sour cream, or whipped cream to the pudding mixture.

Lemon Raisin Pie

Prepare pastry for 2-crust 9-inch pie (see *Pastry*). Pour boiling water over 2 cups raisins and let stand 10 minutes; drain.

Prepare one 3⅝-ounce package *regular* lemon pudding and pie filling mix according to package directions. Stir in 1 tablespoon butter or margarine and raisins. Line 9-inch pie plate with pastry; fill with raisin mixture. Adjust top crust, cutting slits for escape of steam; seal and crimp edge. Bake at 400° till slightly browned, about 35 to 40 minutes.

1-2-3 Apple Pie

    1 21-ounce can French apple pie
        filling
    1 *baked* 9-inch pastry shell
        (See *Pastry*)
    ¾ cup milk
    1 cup dairy sour cream
    1 3¾- or 3⅝-ounce package
        instant vanilla pudding mix
    2 tablespoons sliced, toasted
        almonds

Turn pie filling into pastry shell. Slowly add milk to sour cream; mix well. Add pudding mix; beat according to package directions. Pour over pie filling. Chill. Trim with almonds.

As a change from the common plain pudding or cream pie, try making pudding-based parfaits, frozen desserts, and fancy puddings. The added ingredients dress up the pudding without much extra effort.

Frozen Butterscotch Dream

Combine ⅔ cup sugar, ¼ cup water, 1 egg white, 1 teaspoon lemon juice, and 1 teaspoon vanilla. Beat with electric mixer at high speed till stiff peaks form, about 5 minutes. Whip 1 cup whipping cream; fold into mixture.

Combine one 3⅝- or 4-ounce package *instant* butterscotch pudding mix and 1 cup milk; fold into whipped cream mixture. Add ½ cup chopped walnuts; turn into 10x6x1¾-inch baking dish. Top with ¼ cup chopped walnuts. Freeze 6 to 8 hours or overnight. Serves 6 to 8.

Peach Crumble

    1 cup sugar
    1 beaten egg
    1 cup chopped walnuts
    1 3¾- or 3⅝-ounce package
        instant vanilla pudding mix
    1 cup dairy sour cream
    1 cup milk
    1 cup diced, peeled fresh peaches
        treated with lemon juice

Thoroughly combine first 3 ingredients. Line 15½x10½x1-inch baking pan with foil; grease foil. Spread nut mixture in pan. Bake at 350° till golden brown, about 18 to 20 minutes. Cool; then coarsely crumble. Divide *half* the crumbs among 6 sherbet glasses.

Combine pudding mix, sour cream, and milk; beat till well blended, 1 to 2 minutes. Fold in peaches. Spoon pudding mixture over crumbs in sherbet glasses; top with remaining crumbs. Chill thoroughly. Makes 6 servings.

Lemonade Pudding

    2 slightly beaten egg yolks
    1½ cups milk
    1 3- or 3¼-ounce package *regular*
        vanilla pudding mix
    1 3-ounce package cream cheese,
        softened
    1 6-ounce can frozen lemonade
        concentrate, thawed
    2 egg whites
    ¼ cup sugar
    ½ cup vanilla wafer crumbs
    2 tablespoons chopped walnuts
    2 tablespoons butter, melted

Combine egg yolks and milk. Prepare pudding according to package directions, *using the egg-milk mixture as the liquid*. Add cream cheese and beat smooth with electric or rotary beater; stir in lemonade concentrate. Cover surface with waxed paper and cool 10 minutes; beat smooth again. Beat egg whites to soft peaks; gradually add sugar, beating to stiff peaks. Fold egg whites into pudding. Combine crumbs, nuts, and butter. Sprinkle *half* the crumb mixture into 6 sherbet glasses. Spoon in pudding; top with remaining crumb mixture. Chill the pudding thoroughly. Makes 6 servings.

In the past few years, recipes that use a pudding mix as an ingredient have become popular. Although the pudding loses its identity, the pudding mix adds a delightful flavor to cookies, candies, cakes, and frostings. (See also *Dessert*.)

Unbaked Caramel Cookies

Combine 2 cups sugar, ¾ cup butter or margarine, and one 6-ounce can evaporated milk. Bring mixture to rolling boil, stirring frequently. Remove from heat. Add one 3⅝- or 4-ounce package *instant* butterscotch pudding mix and 3½ cups quick-cooking rolled oats; mix thoroughly. Cool 15 minutes; drop by teaspoonfuls onto waxed paper-lined tray. Makes 60.

Butterscotch Spice Cake

Prepare one 4-ounce package *regular* butterscotch pudding mix according to package directions, *using 2¼ cups milk*. Blend 1 package 2-layer-size spice cake mix into hot pudding (mixture will not be smooth). Pour into lightly greased and floured 13x9x2-inch baking pan. Scatter ½ cup chopped walnuts over batter. Bake at 375° for 25 to 30 minutes. Cut in squares; serve warm or cold with whipped cream or ice cream. Makes 12 to 15 servings.

Easy Chocolate Fudge

½ cup butter or margarine
1 4-ounce package *regular* chocolate pudding mix
1 3- or 3¼-ounce package *regular* vanilla pudding mix
½ cup milk
1 16-ounce package sifted confectioners' sugar
½ teaspoon vanilla
½ cup chopped walnuts

In saucepan melt butter or margarine; stir in dry pudding mixes and milk. Bring to boiling; boil for 1 minute, stirring constantly. Remove from heat; beat in sugar. Stir in vanilla and nuts. Pour into buttered 10x6x1¾-inch baking dish. Garnish with walnut halves, if desired. Chill; cut into squares. Makes 24.

Chocolate Pudding Frosting

1 4-ounce package dark chocolate pudding mix
1¼ cups milk
½ cup butter or margarine
½ cup shortening
1 cup sifted confectioners' sugar
1 teaspoon vanilla
¼ teaspoon salt

Cook pudding according to package directions, *using 1¼ cups milk*. Cover surface of pudding with waxed paper or clear plastic wrap; cool to room temperature. Cream together butter or margarine, shortening, and confectioners' sugar till light and fluffy; stir in vanilla and salt. Gradually beat in cooled chocolate pudding. Frosts two 9-inch layers.

Generous scoops of ice cream melt atop the oven-fresh Date Pudding Cake. This delicious dessert forms two layers as it bakes.

PUDDING CAKE—A dessert that forms a pudding layer and a cake layer as it bakes.

Date Pudding Cake

    1 cup pitted dates
    2 tablespoons butter or margarine
    1 cup boiling water
    1 egg
  1½ cups instant-type flour
   ½ cup granulated sugar
   ½ cup brown sugar
    1 teaspoon baking soda
   ½ teaspoon baking powder
   ½ cup broken walnuts
  1½ cups brown sugar
  1½ cups boiling water
     Vanilla ice cream

Snip dates into a 9-inch round or square baking dish; add butter or margarine. Pour the 1 cup boiling water over; stir to melt butter and soften dates. Add next 7 ingredients and ½ teaspoon salt. Beat with fork till blended, about 2 minutes. Scrape bottom and sides of dish with spatula after 1 minute of beating.

Smooth batter evenly in baking dish; sprinkle with 1½ cups brown sugar. Slowly pour the 1½ cups water over all. Bake at 375° till done, about 40 minutes. Serve warm with scoops of vanilla ice cream piled in center of cake.

Brownie Pudding Cake

    1 cup sifted all-purpose flour
   ¾ cup granulated sugar
    6 tablespoons unsweetened cocoa
      powder
    2 teaspoons baking powder
   ½ cup milk
    2 tablespoons salad oil
    1 teaspoon vanilla
   ¾ cup chopped walnuts
   ¾ cup brown sugar

Sift together flour, granulated sugar, 2 *tablespoons* cocoa, baking powder, and ½ teaspoon salt. Add milk, oil, and vanilla; mix till smooth. Stir in nuts. Pour into greased 8x8x2-inch baking pan. Combine brown sugar, remaining cocoa, and 1¾ cups hot water; pour over batter. Bake at 350° for 45 minutes. Serves 6 to 8.

A light coating of sugar and cinnamon complements the delightful flavor of Applesauce Puffs. They are made with biscuit mix.

PUFF—A light, airy pastry, such as a cream puff, or other food, such as a potato puff.

Potato Puff

Prepare 4 servings packaged instant mashed potatoes according to package directions. Add ½ cup light cream; stir over low heat till very hot. Add 2 tablespoons grated Parmesan cheese, 1 teaspoon instant minced onion, and 1 teaspoon salt. Add 3 egg yolks, one at a time, *beating well after each addition.* Add a little of the hot mixture to 3 stiffly beaten egg whites; fold egg whites into potato mixture. Pour into an *ungreased* 1½-quart casserole. Bake at 375° till knife inserted just off-center comes out clean, about 30 minutes. Serve immediately. Makes 6 servings.

Applesauce Puffs

In mixing bowl combine 2 cups packaged biscuit mix, 1/4 cup sugar, and 1 teaspoon ground cinnamon. Add 1/2 cup applesauce, 1/4 cup milk, 1 slightly beaten egg, and 2 tablespoons salad oil. Beat vigorously for 30 seconds. Fill greased 2-inch muffin pans 2/3 full. Bake at 400° for 12 minutes. Cool slightly; remove muffins from the pans.

Mix 1/4 cup sugar and 1/4 teaspoon ground cinnamon. Melt 2 tablespoons butter or margarine. Dip muffin tops in melted butter, then in sugar-cinnamon mixture. Serve the muffins while they are still warm. Makes 24.

Ginger-Sugar Puffs

      1/4 cup butter, softened
      1/2 cup sugar
      1 egg
      1 teaspoon grated lemon peel
      2 cups sifted all-purpose flour
      4 teaspoons baking powder
      1/2 teaspoon salt
      1/4 teaspoon ground nutmeg
      1 cup milk
      1/2 cup butter or margarine, melted
      3/4 cup sugar
      2 teaspoons ground ginger

Cream 1/4 cup butter and 1/2 cup sugar till light and fluffy; beat in egg and lemon peel. Sift together flour, baking powder, salt, and nutmeg; add to creamed mixture alternately with milk, beating after each addition. Fill small, greased 2-inch muffin pans 2/3 full. Bake at 375° about 15 minutes. While hot, dip muffins quickly into melted butter, then roll in mixture of 3/4 cup sugar and ginger. Makes 36.

PUFFED CEREAL—A ready-to-eat breakfast food made by applying heat and/or pressure to cereal grains until they expand in size and become light and puffy. In 1902 Dr. Alexander P. Anderson, a Columbia University professor, originated the puffing technique by putting rice under pressure in test tubes to explode the starch granules. Puffed wheat and rice were first marketed as breakfast foods in 1909. Now, puffed wheat, rice, corn, and oats are sold.

Butterscotch Cereal Bars

Blend one 3- or 3¼-ounce package *regular* butterscotch pudding mix and 1/2 cup light corn syrup. Heat and stir till boiling. Boil 1/2 minute. Remove from heat; blend in 1/2 cup chunk-style peanut butter. Stir in 4 cups puffed oat cereal till coated. Turn into greased 9x9x 2-inch baking pan. Cool. Makes 18 bars.

PUFF PASTRY—A rich pastry dough that is very flaky when baked. Both the large amount of butter in the dough and the handling technique, which involves rolling butter between layers of dough, contribute to the flakiness of this pastry. Patty shells, Napoleons, fruit-filled turnovers, and Danish pastries are puff pastries.

Flaky Puff Pastry forms the basis for Swiss Cream Torte. Whipped cream, a cream filling, and an icing complete the dessert.

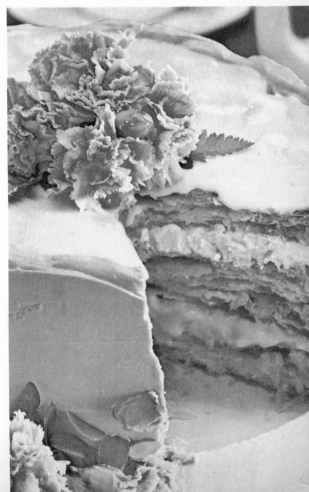

How to roll and fold puff pastry

Follow these pictures for easy Puff Pastry: Roll dough into a rectangle, place chilled butter on half, then fold over as shown.

Press with hand to seal the edge of the dough tightly on three sides. This encloses the layer of butter completely in dough.

Chill the sealed dough thoroughly, at least 1 hour, then roll out to rectangle again. Fold rolled dough evenly into thirds.

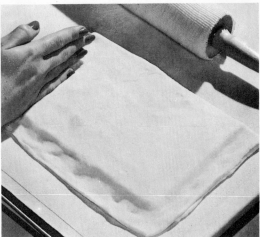

Turn the folded dough and again fold in thirds. Chill thoroughly. Repeat rolling, folding, and chilling 2 or 3 more times.

Puff Pastry

    1 cup butter or margarine
1¾ cups sifted all-purpose flour
  ½ cup ice water

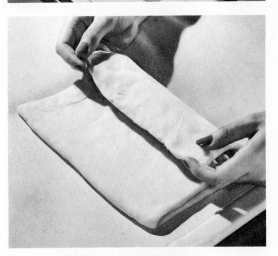

Chill butter or margarine. Reserve 2 tablespoons butter; chill. Work remaining chilled butter with back of wooden spoon just till pliable. Pat or roll between sheets of waxed paper to an 8x6-inch rectangle. Chill at least 1 hour in refrigerator or 20 minutes in freezer. (Chill utensils before each use.)

Cut reserved butter into flour till mixture resembles coarse meal. Add ice water, tossing with fork to make stiff dough. Shape into ball. Knead on *lightly* floured surface till smooth, 5 minutes. Cover; let rest 10 minutes.

On lightly floured surface, roll dough in 15x 9-inch rectangle. Peel waxed paper from one side of chilled butter or margarine; invert on half of dough. Remove remaining waxed paper. Fold dough over to cover butter. Seal edges of dough tightly. Wrap in waxed paper; chill thoroughly, at least 1 hour. Unwrap dough. On *lightly* floured surface, roll to 15x9-inch rectangle. (Roll from center just to edges.) Brush off excess flour; fold in thirds, then turn dough and fold in thirds again. Press edges to seal. Wrap; chill 1 hour. Repeat rolling, folding, and thorough chilling 2 or 3 times more.

Swiss Cream Torte

        Puff Pastry (See page 1801)
    ⅔ cup sugar
    2 tablespoons cornstarch
    ¼ teaspoon salt
    2 cups milk
    3 slightly beaten egg yolks
    1 tablespoon butter or margarine
    1½ teaspoons vanilla
                • • •
    2 cups whipping cream
    ¼ cup sugar
        Red food coloring
    1½ cups sifted confectioners' sugar
    2 tablespoons water

Divide Puff Pastry dough into three parts. Roll each part to a 10-inch circle about ¼ inch thick. (Use inverted dinner plate as pattern; cut around edge with pastry wheel.) Stack circles on *ungreased* baking sheet or tray, separating and covering with waxed paper. Chill thoroughly, 2 to 3 hours or overnight. Remove top circle from refrigerator; place on *ungreased* baking sheet and prick generously. Bake at 350° till light golden brown, about 20 minutes. Repeat with remaining pastry. Cool.

To make cream filling, blend the ⅔ cup sugar, cornstarch, and salt in saucepan. Gradually stir in milk. Cook, stirring constantly, till mixture thickens and bubbles. Remove from heat. Gradually stir small amount of hot mixture into egg yolks; return to hot mixture. Cook 2 minutes more, stirring constantly. Remove the mixture from heat; add butter or margarine and *1 teaspoon* of the vanilla. Cool.

Whip cream and the ¼ cup sugar together till stiff. Add enough food coloring to *half* of whipped cream to tint pink. Set aside. For icing, blend together confectioners' sugar, water, and remaining vanilla till smooth.

To assemble torte: Place one layer of Puff Pastry on serving plate; spread evenly with cooled cream filling. Spread another layer of pastry with untinted whipped cream and gently place atop the first layer. Top with remaining layer, bottom side up. Spread icing evenly over top of torte. Frost sides with tinted whipped cream, building up a slight rim at top edge. Chill at least 2 hours before serving. If desired, garnish with a wide band of toasted, sliced almonds and sugared flowers. To serve, cut in wedges. Makes about 12 servings.

PUFFY—Light and airy. Foods such as soufflés and cream puffs become puffy as the air bubbles expand during baking.

PULLED CANDY—Noncrystalline candy, such as taffy, made from a cooled sugar syrup. At the right stage, the candy is pulled till light in color and porous. (See *Candy, Taffy* for additional information.)

Vanilla Taffy

    3 cups sugar
    1 cup light corn syrup
    ¾ cup boiling water
    ¼ cup vinegar
    ½ teaspoon cream of tartar
    1 tablespoon vanilla

In large saucepan combine first 4 ingredients. Cook and stir till mixture reaches rolling boil. Stir in cream of tartar. Cook to hard-ball stage (265°). Remove from heat; stir in vanilla. Pour into buttered 15½x10½x1-inch pan. Cool till comfortable to handle. Butter hands; gather taffy into ball. Divide in half and *immediately* pull with fingertips till candy is light in color and hard to pull. Divide each piece in half. Quickly pull each piece into ½-inch thick strand and twist. With buttered scissors, quickly snip into pieces. Wrap with waxed paper.

PULLET—A young, usually under one-year-old hen. (See also *Chicken.*)

PULQUE (*pōōl' kē*)—A Mexican alcoholic beverage made by fermenting agave juice.

PULSE—An old-fashioned name for legumes, such as beans. (See also *Legumes.*)

PUMPERNICKEL (*pum' puhr nik' uhl*)—A dark, heavy, European-style rye bread. Dark molasses, caraway seeds, and rye flour give pumpernickel its characteristic flavor. To give the bread structure, all-purpose white flour is added to the rye flour.

Several types of pumpernickel—medium-dark, dark, and very dark—are frequently available on the market. As a general rule, the darker the pumpernickel, the more sour the taste and chewy the texture.

Pumpernickel Bread

A favorite bread for sandwiches—

> 3 packages active dry yeast
> 1½ cups warm water
> ½ cup dark molasses
> 1 to 2 tablespoons caraway seed
> 1 tablespoon salt
> 2 tablespoons shortening
> 2¾ cups stirred rye flour
> 2¼ to 2¾ cups sifted all-purpose flour

Soften active dry yeast in *warm* water (110°). Combine molasses, caraway seed, salt, shortening, rye flour, about *1 cup* of the all-purpose flour, and the softened yeast. Beat till smooth. Add enough remaining flour to make a stiff dough. Turn out on lightly floured surface and knead till smooth and elastic (8 to 10 minutes). Place dough in greased bowl, turning once to grease surface. Cover and let rise in warm place till double, about 1½ hours.

Punch down and divide dough into 2 parts. Cover and let rest 10 minutes. Round each part into a smooth ball. Place on opposite corners of a cornmeal-sprinkled baking sheet. Cover and let rise till double, about 30 minutes. Bake loaves at 375° till well browned, about 30 to 35 minutes. For a chewy crust, brush tops of the loaves with warm water several times during the baking, after the first 20 minutes. Makes 2 round loaves of bread.

Peanut Butter-Bacon Sandwich

An easy-to-make, delicious filling sandwiched between slices of pumpernickel bread—

> ½ cup peanut butter
> 6 slices bacon, crisp-cooked, drained, and crumbled
> ⅓ cup finely chopped celery
> 10 slices pumpernickel bread, toasted and buttered
> Lettuce

Combine peanut butter, crumbled bacon, and celery. Spread 5 slices toasted pumpernickel with peanut butter mixture, using about 3 tablespoons mixture for each; top with lettuce and remaining slices of buttered pumpernickel toast. Makes 5 sandwiches.

PUMPKIN—A large, oval to round, golden yellow to orange vegetable belonging to the gourd family and related to squash, muskmelons, and cucumbers. Pumpkins generally vary in weight from a few pounds to 30 pounds, but hundred-pound pumpkins are not at all uncommon. For many years, pumpkins were called *pompions*, an old French word derived from the Greek meaning "cooked by the sun."

Native to tropical America, pumpkins were first used by the Indians and became an integral part of the early American culture. It didn't take the Pilgrim homemakers long to learn from the Indians how to make pumpkin a good-tasting, popular food. Although it's doubtful that they served pumpkin pie at the first Thanksgiving, pumpkin in one form or another was certainly part of that well-known feast.

Pumpkins were utilized to such a great extent by these early settlers that an unknown writer in about 1630 remarked, "We have pumpkins at morning, and pumpkins at noon. If it were not for pumpkins, we should be undone." Pumpkins were often dried for year-round use.

In either form, pumpkins were used in a variety of ways. Stewed pumpkin was mixed with Indian meal for bread. A simple pumpkin pudding was made by slicing off the top of a small pumpkin, scooping out seeds and fibers, and filling the hollow with milk. With the top replaced, the pumpkin was baked in its shell until the milk was absorbed by the softened pulp. The hollowed-out pumpkin was often filled and baked with a spiced apple stuffing, too.

It is not known when the first pumpkin pie was served, although family recipes for it have been passed from mother to daughter for many generations. By the time Amelia Simmons published the first recipe for pumpkin pie in 1796, however, this dessert had become the traditional last course of a Thanksgiving dinner.

Pumpkins are not limited to America alone. In China, pumpkins were considered symbols of success and health. When introduced to Europe, pumpkins were called Turkey cucumbers because they had come by way of Turkey. The French later established a September Festival of King Pumpkin at the Paris produce market.

Two favorite pies merge into one for Two-Tone Holiday Pie.
Atop the mincemeat layer rests a velvety pumpkin custard.
A wreath of whipped cream piping decorates the pie.

Nutritional value: The greatest contribution of pumpkin to the diet is in the form of vitamin A. One-half cup of cooked pumpkin provides more than the day's recommended allowance for this vitamin as well as smaller amounts of other vitamins and minerals. Although this half-cup portion contains only about 40 calories, it is usually combined with sweet or dessert-type ingredients that increase the caloric content of the recipe.

How to select and store: The largest percentage of fresh pumpkins are marketed in October. But because of the lengthy preparation time required for fresh pumpkin, a large share of the pumpkin used today has been processed in cans.

When choosing fresh pumpkins, select small-sized, heavy ones since they have less waste and more tender flesh than do the larger pumpkins. Save the large ones for Halloween jack-o-lanterns. Also look for pumpkins that are vivid in color, firm, and have a minimum of blemishes.

Stored in a cool, dry area, pumpkins can be kept for several months. Be sure that they are never allowed to freeze.

How to prepare and use: Whether you serve fresh pumpkin as a vegetable or use it with other foods, it must always be cooked. Wash the pumpkin, cut it in half, and scrape out the seeds and fibrous material. Cut in cubes and peel. Then, cook it in boiling, salted water till tender.

As a vegetable, butter the cooked cubes and season with spices or herbs. Or mash the pumpkin and season it like squash.

Regardless of its intended use—traditional pumpkin pie, a pumpkin pie variation, pudding, custard, bread, cookie, or cake—you'll find the flavor of pumpkin pleasing. (See also *Vegetable*.)

Pumpkin Pie

A classic recipe—

 1½ cups canned pumpkin
 ¾ cup sugar
 ½ teaspoon salt
 1 to 1¼ teaspoons ground
   cinnamon
 ½ to 1 teaspoon ground ginger
 ¼ to ½ teaspoon ground nutmeg
 ¼ to ½ teaspoon ground cloves
       • • •
 3 slightly beaten eggs
 1¼ cups milk
 1 6-ounce can evaporated milk
   (⅔ cup)
 1 *unbaked* 9-inch pastry shell
   (See *Pastry*)

Combine pumpkin, sugar, salt, cinnamon, ginger, nutmeg, and cloves. Blend in eggs, milk, and evaporated milk. Pour into pastry shell (have edges crimped high because amount of filling is generous). Bake at 400° till knife inserted halfway between center and edge comes out clean, about 50 minutes. Cool thoroughly.

Two-Tone Holiday Pie

A mincemeat-pumpkin combo—

 1½ cups canned mincemeat
 1 *unbaked* 9-inch pastry shell
   (See *Pastry*)
 1 18-ounce can pumpkin pie
   filling
 ¼ cup orange juice
 1 cup evaporated milk
 ½ teaspoon grated orange peel
       • • •
   Whipped cream *or* dessert
   topping

Spread mincemeat evenly in bottom of unbaked pastry shell. Prepare pumpkin pie filling following label directions, *substituting the orange juice and evaporated milk for the liquid called for;* stir in orange peel. Pour pumpkin mixture over mincemeat in pastry shell.

Bake the pie in a 400° oven till a knife inserted halfway between center and edge of the filling comes out clean, about 45 minutes. Cool the pie thoroughly. Serve the pie garnished with a ring of rosettes made with whipped cream or whipped dessert topping.

Pumpkin Cookies

Equally good plain or frosted—

 1 cup shortening
 1 cup sugar
 1 egg
 1 cup canned pumpkin
 1 teaspoon vanilla
       • • •
 2 cups sifted all-purpose flour
 1 teaspoon baking powder
 ½ teaspoon baking soda
 ½ teaspoon salt
 1 teaspoon ground cinnamon
 ½ teaspoon ground nutmeg
 ¼ teaspoon ground allspice
       • • •
 1 cup raisins
 ½ cup chopped nuts
   Butter Frosting (optional)

Thoroughly cream shortening and sugar together. Add egg, pumpkin, and vanilla; beat well. Sift together flour, baking powder, baking soda, salt, cinnamon, nutmeg, and allspice. Add to creamed mixture; blend well. Stir in raisins and nuts. Drop by rounded teaspoons, 2 inches apart, on greased cookie sheet. Bake at 350° for 12 to 15 minutes. Remove from sheet. Frost immediately with Butter Frosting, if desired. Makes about 3½ dozen cookies.

Butter Frosting: Cream 3 tablespoons butter or margarine; gradually add 1¼ cups sifted confectioners' sugar, blending well. Beat in 1 tablespoon light cream and ½ teaspoon vanilla. Gradually blend in another 1¼ cups sifted confectioners' sugar. Add enough light cream (about 1 tablespoon) to sugar mixture to make frosting of spreading consistency.

Pumpkin-Raisin Loaves

    ¾ cup canned pumpkin
    ⅓ cup water
    1 egg
    1 teaspoon pumpkin pie spice
    1 14-ounce package apple–cinnamon
        muffin mix
    ½ cup raisins
        • • •
    Milk
    2 cups sifted confectioners' sugar

In mixing bowl combine canned pumpkin,
water, egg, and pumpkin pie spice. Add apple-
cinnamon muffin mix and raisins; stir just till
moistened. Turn batter into 3 greased 5½x3x2-
inch loaf pans (or one 9x5x3-inch loaf pan).
Bake at 350° for 35 to 40 minutes for small
loaves or 50 minutes for large loaf. Turn bread
from loaf pans; cool on rack.

   To make icing, add enough milk to the sifted
confectioners' sugar to make of pouring consistency. Drizzle icing over cooled loaves.

Golden Pumpkin Muffins

In mixing bowl thoroughly combine 2 cups
packaged biscuit mix, ½ cup sugar, and 1½
teaspoons pumpkin pie spice. In small bowl
combine ¾ cup milk, ½ cup canned pumpkin,
1 slightly beaten egg, and 2 tablespoons salad
oil; stir into dry ingredients till blended. Fill
greased muffin cups ⅔ full. Bake at 400° about
20 minutes. Makes 1 dozen muffins.

PUNCH—An alcoholic or nonalcoholic beverage that frequently contains fruit juice.
Punch differs from most other beverages
in that it has a combination of flavors
rather than one predominating flavor.
Punch is usually made in quantities suf-
ficient to accommodate a large crowd.

   The name punch comes from the Hindu
word for "five," which originally referred
to the number of ingredients in this popular beverage. A typical early punch that
bore out this rule of five contained spirits,
lemon juice, sugar, water, and spices. This
is no longer the case, however, today, there
are numerous punches that contain many
more than five ingredients.

For ice ring, fill the mold half full of water.
Freeze firm as quickly as possible. Arrange
fruit and leaves. Anchor by pouring a small
amount of water around them; freeze.

At serving time, carefully unmold the pretty
ice ring by loosening bottom with hot, wet
cloth or by dipping it in cold water. Float
ice ring, fruit side up, atop punch.

Punch is usually served by ladling it from a large bowl into small cups. In fact, punch bowl sets, which include matching cups and a ladle, are customarily used.

If the punch is to be served cold, use cold ingredients and add a block or ring of ice to the punch bowl. Besides keeping the punch cold, the ice serves as a garnish if you place the water in a mold or ice tray and freeze flowers, fruit pieces, mint sprigs, or other decorative foods in the ice. (See also *Beverage*.)

Popfreeze Punch

  1 envelope unsweetened raspberry-
     flavored soft drink powder
½ cup sugar
  4 cups pineapple juice
       . . .
  4 7-ounce bottles lemon-lime
     carbonated beverage (about
     1 quart)

Combine raspberry-flavored soft drink powder, sugar, and pineapple juice. Freeze in two ice cube trays. Remove cubes and store in plastic bag in freezer.* To serve place ice cubes in glasses; fill with lemon-lime beverage; stir to blend flavors. Makes about 8 servings.

*For an outdoor meal, pack ice cubes (in plastic bag) in insulated picnic cooler—they will stay frozen for about 3 hours.

Spiced Percolator Punch

  9 cups pineapple juice
  9 cups cranberry juice cocktail
4½ cups water
  1 cup brown sugar
     . . .
4½ teaspoons whole cloves
  4 cinnamon sticks, broken in
     pieces
¼ teaspoon salt

Combine pineapple juice, cranberry juice cocktail, water, and brown sugar in 30-cup automatic coffee maker. Place cloves, cinnamon stick pieces, and salt in coffee-maker basket. Assemble coffee maker; plug in and perk. Serve piping hot. Makes about 23 cups.

Warm Cranberry Punch

2½ quarts cranberry juice cocktail
  5 cups water
½ cup sugar
½ cup light raisins
  1 tablespoon shredded orange peel
  2 medium oranges, studded with
     whole cloves

In saucepan combine cranberry juice cocktail, water, sugar, raisins, and orange peel. Add clove-studded oranges. Cover and simmer 10 minutes. Serve warm. Makes about 25 servings.

Tropical Punch

  1 large watermelon
  1 46-ounce can red Hawaiian
     fruit punch (about 6 cups)
  1 6-ounce can frozen pink
     lemonade concentrate
  1 6-ounce can frozen orange juice
     concentrate
  1 6-ounce can frozen pineapple
     juice concentrate
  6 cups cold water
     . . .
  1 28-ounce bottle ginger ale,
     chilled (3½ cups)
  Orange and lime slices

Stand watermelon on end; cut thin slice off bottom to make it level. Cut top third off melon. Using cup as guide, trace scallops around top outside edge of melon. Carve scalloped edge, following pattern. Scoop out fruit; serve later. Chill melon shell.

Combine Hawaiian fruit punch, fruit juice concentrates, and water. Pour over ice in melon bowl. Resting bottle on rim of melon, carefully pour ginger ale down side; mix with an up-and-down motion. Float orange and lime slices. Twine melon with ivy leaves, holding with wooden picks. Makes 30 to 35 servings.

1-2-3 Easy Party Punch

Combine one 6-ounce can frozen orange juice concentrate, thawed, and ⅓ cup light corn syrup. Add one 28-ounce bottle ginger ale, chilled. Pour over ice in bowl. Serves 10.

Lemon Punch

2 cups sugar
4 teaspoons grated lemon peel
1 cup lemon juice
1 to 2 pints lemon sherbet
1 to 2 pints orange sherbet
2 28-ounce bottles ginger ale, chilled

In saucepan combine sugar and 2 cups water. Heat and stir till sugar dissolves; cool. Add 2 cups water, lemon peel, and juice; chill. Pour into chilled punch bowl; add scoops of sherbet, stirring till partially melted. Pour chilled ginger ale down side of bowl, stirring with an up-and-down motion. Serve *immediately* in punch cups. Makes 4 quarts.

Lime Frosted Punch

3½ to 4 cups pineapple-grapefruit drink, chilled
⅔ cup lemon juice
2 quarts cold water
3 ½-ounce envelopes unsweetened lemon-lime soft drink powder
2 cups sugar
2 pints lime sherbet
4 7-ounce bottles lemon-lime carbonated beverage, chilled

In punch bowl combine fruit juices, water, soft drink powder, and sugar. Stir till soft drink powder and sugar are completely dissolved. Top with large spoonfuls of sherbet. Resting bottle on rim of bowl, carefully pour in carbonated beverage. Serve some sherbet with each cup. Makes 30 to 35 servings.

Mock Champagne Punch

In punch bowl combine one 6-ounce can frozen lemonade concentrate, one 6-ounce can frozen pineapple juice concentrate, and 2 cups cold water. Float ice ring or cubes containing fresh mint leaves and maraschino cherries on top. Carefully pour two 7-ounce bottles ginger ale, chilled; two 7-ounce bottles sparkling water, chilled; and 1 large bottle *sparkling* Catawba grape juice (white), chilled, down side of punch bowl. Makes 11 cups.

Sparkle Punch

1 ½-ounce envelope unsweetened lemon-lime *or* cherry-flavored soft drink powder
1 cup sugar
2 cups cold milk
1 quart vanilla ice cream
1 28-ounce bottle carbonated water (3½ cups)

Combine soft drink powder and sugar. Dissolve in milk. Pour into 6 to 8 soda glasses. Add scoops of ice cream. Resting bottle on rim of glass, carefully pour in carbonated water to fill. Stir to muddle slightly. Serves 6 to 8.

Frosty Party Punch

2 3-ounce packages raspberry-flavored gelatin
1 3-ounce package cherry-flavored gelatin
3 cups boiling water
2 12-ounce cans pineapple juice, chilled
1 12-ounce can frozen orange juice concentrate
1 1-quart tray ice cubes
2 pints pineapple *or* lemon sherbet

Dissolve raspberry- and cherry-flavored gelatins in boiling water. Add 5 cups cold water, pineapple juice, and orange juice concentrate.* Stir in ice cubes just till melted. Spoon in sherbet. Serve immediately. Serves 32.

*If desired, prepare this mixture several hours ahead; keep at room temperature. Just before serving, add ice and sherbet.

Cranberry Punch

1 16-ounce can jellied cranberry sauce
¾ cup orange juice
¼ cup lemon juice
1 28-ounce bottle ginger ale (3½ cups), chilled

Beat jellied cranberry sauce till smooth. Stir in orange and lemon juice. Add ginger ale. Serve over ice. Makes 12 to 15 servings.

Quantity Fruit Punch

Makes enough for 75 people—

      3 quarts pineapple juice
  1½ cups lemon juice
      3 cups orange juice
   ⅓ cup lime juice
  2½ cups sugar
      1 cup lightly packed fresh mint
         leaves
                • • •
      4 28-ounce bottles ginger ale
      2 28-ounce bottles carbonated
         water
      1 pint fresh strawberries,
         quartered

Combine juices, sugar, and mint; chill. Just before serving, add ginger ale, carbonated water, and strawberries; pour over cake of ice in punch bowl. Makes 75 servings.

Hot Lemon Punch

   1 cup sugar
   5 cups water
   1 cup lemon juice
   1 cup gin
      Lemon slices

In saucepan combine sugar, water, and lemon juice. Cook, stirring constantly, till sugar is dissolved and mixture just begins to boil. Add gin; heat through. Pour into punch bowl. Float lemon slices on top. Makes 7½ cups.

Burgundy Punch

   2 fifths Burgundy
   2 cups port wine
   2 cups orange juice
  ¼ cup lemon juice
   1 cup sugar
   1 quart water
   2 quarts ice cubes

Combine Burgundy, port, orange juice, and lemon juice. Stir in sugar and water and mix well. Chill till serving time. Just before serving, pour over 2 quarts ice cubes (3 to 4 trays) in punch bowl. Makes about 4 quarts.

PUNGENT—A flavor or aroma that is so strong it causes a warm, prickly sensation in the mouth or nose. For example, limburger cheese and highly spiced Mexican foods have pungent flavors and aromas.

PURÉE (*pyŏŏ rā,'-rē', pyŏŏr'ā*)—**1.** To reduce a food to a smooth pulp. A cooked or a soft, raw food can be puréed by removing all seeds, then pushing the food through a sieve or whirling it in a blender. **2.** A smooth soup made from vegetable pulp.

PURI (*pû' rē*)—Small, individual breads of India that are deep-fat fried. Puris make an interesting and delicious curry accompaniment. (See also *Indian Cookery*.)

PURIS

   2 tablespoons shortening
   2 cups sifted all-purpose flour
  ½ teaspoon salt
   2 ounces sharp process American
      cheese, shredded (½ cup)
  ½ to ⅔ cup water

In mixing bowl cut shortening into flour and salt. Add cheese. Stir in water to make a soft dough. Knead and pound dough for about 10 to 15 minutes. Cover and let stand ½ hour. Roll *very thin* on lightly floured surface. Cut in 4-inch circles. Fry in deep, hot fat (400°) till puffed and golden, turning once. Drain on towels. Keep them warm in very slow oven, or warm just before serving time. Makes 12.

PURPLE BASIL—A variety of the herb basil that is characterized by dark reddish purple leaves. Like other basil, purple basil has a pleasant, spicy flavor and aroma. This herb is especially delightful in green salads since it adds color as well as flavor. (See also *Basil*.)

PURSLANE (*pûrs' lān,-lin*)—A plant characterized by thick, fleshy leaves and a reddish green stem. Although purslane can be cultivated, it more often grows wild.

The young leaves, which can be cooked like spinach, have a slightly tart flavor. The crisp stem is sometimes pickled.

Q

QUAHOG *(kwô′ hog, -hôg, kwuh hog′, -hôg′)*—Another name for the edible hard-shell clam. Quahog is an Indian word that is used primarily in the New England area. (See also *Clam.*)

QUAIL—A game bird that is highly esteemed for its culinary uses. The American quail belongs to the partridge family.

The elusive American quail, most commonly known as the bobwhite, is a non-migratory bird and is considered by many sportsmen to be the most cunning of all game birds. As an example of this natural cleverness, when quail group, they huddle in a circle, facing out, which serves two purposes: warmth and protection. And when "flushed" the birds scatter into many different directions to the dismay of the predator.

This type of quail nests on the ground, and it seems to perfer running rather than flying. The latter characteristic would ordinarily rule it out as a game bird, but the bobwhite's ability to conceal itself by means of a reddish brown coloring and its habit of "freezing" (remaining motionless when in danger of discovery) make it a challenging bird to hunt.

There are also varieties of quail common to Europe, Asia, and Africa. Many of these birds are migratory and were known to people of ancient lands. The Egyptians are said to have exported quail to other countries. Some Biblical scholars believe that the manna that was miraculously sent to the wandering Israelites consisted partially of migrating quail.

A quail should be properly handled after it is killed and should be cleaned immediately. When cooked, quail has a delicate flavor. This is due in part to the diet of the bird—berries, insects, and seeds. The meat is often dry and needs to be basted with butter or kept moist with fat during cooking. Broil or roast young birds.

Whole quail can be purchased frozen and canned. Smoked meat and quail eggs are considered gourmet items. (See also *Game.*)

Broiled Quail

> 4 4- to 6-ounce ready-to-cook quail,
>   split in halves lengthwise
> ½ cup butter or margarine, melted
>   Salt and pepper

Brush quail with melted butter or margarine; season with salt and pepper. Place, skin side up, on broiler pan (no rack). Broil about 5 minutes in a preheated broiler 4 to 5 inches from heat. Turn; broil 6 to 9 minutes. Brush frequently with melted butter or margarine during broiling. Remove to warm serving platter. Garnish with parsley and serve with currant jelly, if desired. Makes 4 servings.

How to roast quail

Salt inside of ready-to-cook 4- to 6-ounce quail. Stuff as desired; truss bird. Place, breast side up, on rack in shallow roasting pan. Place bacon slices over breast. Roast, uncovered, at 400° till tender, allowing 30 to 45 minutes. (Timing may vary, depending on age of the bird; young birds are the most suitable for roasting.) Baste occasionally with drippings. When necessary, place foil loosely over top of bird to prevent excess browning. Allow ½ to 1 pound quail for each serving.

QUANTITY COOKERY—A type of food preparation that is geared towards feeding a large number of people. Cooking for restaurants and other establishments as well as the cooking that homemakers do for church groups, large family gatherings, clubs, and organizations are included in this type of food preparation. However, restaurant cooking is a specialized business using quantity equipment and supplies not often available for home use.

Homemakers who cook for large groups know that it takes special planning to have everything ready at the designated serving time. Even if you're not the type of person who normally makes lists, your job will be easier if you write down deadlines and tasks to be completed.

The first step in planning for large-group entertaining is determining the guest list. This should help you decide whether to serve a buffet or a sit-down meal. You might also keep in mind friends you can call on for help. When you have some helpers, you can generally plan a more elaborate menu for your guests.

Next, plan what you'll want to serve, keeping in mind proper menu planning techniques. Be sure that the foods selected are varied in texture, temperature, flavor, color, size, and shape. Also consider the likes and dislikes of the group.

Another important consideration in planning for large groups is determining the amount of equipment that will be needed. If you don't have enough plates, flatware, or glasses on hand, paper or plastic items can be used for informal occasions. For more formal occasions, rent matching dishes. And don't overlook limitations in oven and refrigerator space as well as in the mixing and baking pans.

Keep the menu as uncomplicated as possible, but plan to have plenty of food on hand for seconds. Casseroles or one-dish meals are good choices for quantity serving. Both food preparation and serving are simplified with one main dish. To complete the meal, simply add a salad, bread, beverage, and dessert. Another advantage of casserole main dishes is that they can be prepared ahead of time and kept in the refrigerator. However, be sure to allow extra cooking time for the chilled casserole to heat through.

Although some recipes can be doubled or tripled successfully, others such as baked goods, which have balanced formulas, just don't adapt well to quantity cookery. Mixing and baking times as well as the seasoning balance can be affected by multiplying recipes. Therefore, unless the recipe is geared to quantity cookery, it is best to make several batches.

Many of the casserole recipes that follow are made in two 13x9x2-inch pans. However, you can substitute one 18x12x2½-inch baking pan if one is available. Be sure to allow two inches of space around the pan for even heat circulation.

When the final plans are completed and you know what you want to serve, make out a detailed market order including all cleanup supplies that will be needed. You may be able to purchase some food items in institution-sized containers from a wholesaler or restaurant supplier. If you're going to need any special items, be sure you know where they are available, and give advance notice so that you will be able to obtain the quantities you need.

When it comes time to prepare the food, do as much as possible ahead of time to eliminate last-minute work, especially if you are the only chef. You'll find that the freezer can be put to good use for make-ahead desserts, salads, and breads. Also have dishes used for food preparation washed so that there will be plenty of counter space for serving.

If you are fortunate enough to have some helpers, assign to each of them a specific task—making a batch of a specified recipe, helping with the table setting and decorations, or cleaning up the dining area after the meal has been served. Advance notice should be given to each helper so that she is informed of her task. well ahead of time. (See *Buffet, Meal Planning* for additional information.)

Hamburger-Noodle Bake

      4 pounds ground beef
      3 cups chopped onion
          . . .
     16 ounces medium noodles, cooked
          and drained
     16 ounces sharp process American
          cheese, shredded (4 cups)
      3 10¾-ounce cans condensed
          tomato soup
      3 cups water
     ¾ cup chopped green pepper
     ½ cup chili sauce
     ¼ cup chopped canned pimiento
     1½ teaspoons salt
          Dash pepper
          . . .
      3 cups soft bread crumbs
      6 tablespoons butter or margarine,
          melted
          Green pepper rings

Divide beef and onion between 2 large skillets. Brown meat. Drain off fat. Combine meat and onion with cooked noodles, cheese, soup, water, green pepper, chili sauce, pimiento, salt, and pepper. Mix the ingredients well.

Turn ingredients into *two* 13x9x2-inch baking dishes. Combine soft bread crumbs and melted butter or margarine. Sprinkle atop casseroles. Bake, uncovered, at 350° till hot, about 40 to 45 minutes. Trim the casseroles with green pepper rings. Makes 25 to 30 servings.

For serving a crowd

← When it's your turn to bring a casserole for the church supper or family gathering, prepare the popular Hamburger-Noodle Bake.

Spanish Rice

      1 pound sliced bacon
      2 cups chopped onion
      2 cups chopped green pepper
      2 28-ounce cans tomatoes
      5 cups water
      1 pound uncooked packaged pre-
          cooked rice (5 cups)
      1 cup chili sauce
      1 tablespoon salt
     ¼ teaspoon pepper
      1 tablespoon brown sugar
      2 teaspoons Worcestershire sauce
      8 ounces sharp process American
          cheese, shredded (2 cups)

Cook bacon till crisp; drain. Pour off all but ½ cup bacon fat. In remaining fat, cook onion and green pepper till tender. Add remaining ingredients except cheese. Pour mixture into *two* 13x9x2-inch baking dishes. Cover; bake at 350° till rice is done, about 25 to 30 minutes. Crumble bacon; sprinkle each dish with *half* the bacon, then cheese. Return to oven to melt cheese. Makes 25 servings.

Macaroni and Cheese

     1¼ pounds elbow macaroni (6 cups)
     ¾ cup butter or margarine
     ½ cup sifted all-purpose flour
      2 teaspoons salt
     ¼ teaspoon pepper
     10 cups milk
      1 cup chopped onion (optional)
     1½ pounds sharp process American
          cheese, cubed (6 cups)
      4 tomatoes, sliced

In two large kettles cook macaroni in large amount of boiling, salted water till tender; drain. In large kettle melt butter; blend in flour, salt, and pepper. Add milk; cook and stir the mixture till it is thickened and bubbly. Add onion and cheese; stir till cheese is melted. Spread macaroni in *two* 13x9x2-inch metal baking pans. Add *half* the sauce to each pan; mix with macaroni. Sprinkle tomato slices with salt; arrange them on top, pushing edge of each slice into macaroni. Bake at 350° till bubbly and hot in center, about 45 minutes. Makes 24 (about ¾ cup) servings.

Italian Meat Sauce

In two large kettles or Dutch ovens combine 4 pounds ground beef; 4 large onions, chopped; and 8 cloves garlic, minced. Brown the ingredients lightly. Drain off the excess fat. Divide the following ingredients evenly between the two kettles: six 30-ounce cans tomatoes, undrained and broken up; four 6-ounce cans tomato paste; 8 cups water; 1 cup snipped parsley; 1/4 cup brown sugar; 2 tablespoons ground oregano; 1 tablespoon salt; 1 teaspoon dried thyme leaves, crushed; and 4 bay leaves.

Simmer, uncovered, till sauce is thickened, about 3 hours; stir occasionally. Remove bay leaves. Cook 3 to 4 pounds spaghetti. Serve sauce over spaghetti. Pass shredded Parmesan cheese. Makes 25 (3/4 cup) servings.

Chili Con Carne

    4 pounds ground beef
    1 tablespoon salt
    4 large onions, chopped (4 cups)
    4 medium green peppers, chopped
    4 16-ounce cans kidney beans,
        drained
    2 29-ounce cans tomatoes
    2 15-ounce cans tomato sauce
 1 1/2 to 2 tablespoons chili powder
  1/2 teaspoon paprika
    3 bay leaves, finely crushed

Season ground beef with salt. Brown the meat in a 10-quart Dutch oven or kettle. Add onion and green pepper; cook till tender but not brown. Add the remaining ingredients. Cover and simmer for 2 hours, stirring occasionally. Add water if needed for desired consistency. Makes 25 (about 1 cup) servings.

Cabbage Slaw

Combine 2 1/4 pounds cabbage, shredded (15 cups); 3/4 pound carrots, shredded (3 cups); and 3/4 cup diced green pepper; chill. Blend together 3 cups mayonnaise or salad dressing, 1/3 cup sugar, 1/3 cup vinegar, 1 tablespoon prepared mustard, 3 teaspoons celery seed, and 2 teaspoons salt. Just before serving the slaw, toss the vegetables and the mayonnaise mixture lightly. Makes 25 (1/2 cup) servings.

Roaster Baked Beans

    8 31-ounce cans pork and beans
        in tomato sauce
    2 14-ounce bottles catsup
    1 large onion, chopped (1 cup)
  1/2 pound brown sugar (1 1/4 cups)
    2 tablespoons dry mustard
    1 pound bacon, cut in pieces

Empty cans of pork and beans into inset pan of electric roaster, preheated to 300°. Stir next 4 ingredients into beans. Sprinkle bacon pieces over. Cook, covered, at 300° for 2 hours. Uncover and continue cooking 2 hours, stirring occasionally. Makes 25 servings.

Punch for the Crowd

    3 quarts pineapple juice
 1 1/2 cups lemon juice
    3 cups orange juice
  1/3 cup lime juice
 2 1/2 cups sugar
    1 cup mint leaves
    4 28-ounce bottles ginger ale,
        chilled
    2 28-ounce bottles carbonated
        water, chilled
    1 pint fresh strawberries, sliced

Combine juices, sugar, and mint leaves; chill. Strain. Pour over large cake of ice in punch bowl. Carefully pour in ginger ale and carbonated water; add berries. Serves 75.

Tossed Green Salad

    3 heads iceberg lettuce
    1 bunch romaine
    2 bunches radishes, sliced
    2 large cucumbers, thinly sliced
    2 large green peppers, chopped
    1 large onion, chopped (optional)
    1 pint French dressing
  2/3 cup sweet pickle relish
  1/3 cup vinegar

Tear lettuce and romaine in pieces. Combine with next 4 ingredients. Chill. Combine remaining ingredients. Pour over salad before serving. Toss. Makes 25 (about 1 cup) servings.

Guide To Shopping For A Crowd

Use this table as a guide when planning and shopping for food for a large group. The size of one serving (Serving Unit) is listed for each item. For hearty eaters, plan about 1½ servings for each person.

Food	Servings	Serving Unit	Amount Needed
Beverages			
Coffee	25	1 cup	½ to ¾ pound
Tea, hot	25	1 cup	1 ounce
Tea, iced	25	1 glass	3 ounces
Cream, coffee	25	1 tablespoon	1 pint
Milk	24	1 8-ounce glass	1½ gallons
Breads and Cereals			
Biscuits	25	2 ounces	4½ dozen
Bread	25	1-ounce slice	1¼ pounds
Rice, long-grain	24	½ cup, cooked	1½ pounds, uncooked
Rolls	24	1	2 dozen
Spaghetti	25	¾ cup, cooked	2¼ pounds, uncooked
Desserts			
Cake	24	1/12 cake	2 9-inch layer cakes
	24	2½-inch square	1 15½x10½x1-inch sheet
Ice Cream	24	½ cup or 1 slice	3 quarts
Pie	30	1/6 pie	5 9-inch pies
Fruit			
Canned	24	½ cup	1 6½- to 7¼-pound can
Relishes			
Carrot strips	25	2 to 3 strips	1 to 1¼ pounds
Cauliflowerets	25	2 ounces sliced, raw	7 pounds
Celery	25	1 2- to 3-inch piece	1 medium stalk
Olives	25	3 to 4	1 quart
Pickles	25	1 ounce	1 quart
Radishes	25	2	5 bunches
Salads			
Side Dish:			
Cottage cheese	25	⅓ cup	5 pounds
Fruit	24	⅓ cup	2 quarts
Gelatin	25	½ cup liquid	3 quarts
Potato	24	½ cup	3 quarts
Tossed vegetable	25	¾ cup	5 quarts
Main Dish	25	1 cup	6¼ quarts
Soup	25	1 cup (main course)	2 50-ounce cans condensed
Vegetables			
Canned	25	½ cup	1 6½- to 7¼-pound can
Fresh:			
Potatoes	25	½ cup, mashed	6¾ pounds
	25	1 medium, baked	8½ pounds
Frozen:			
Beans	25	⅓ cup	5¼ pounds
Carrots, peas, or corn	25	⅓ cup	5 pounds
Potatoes, French-fried	25	10 pieces	3¼ pounds
Miscellaneous			
Butter	32	1 pat	½ pound
Jam or preserves	25	2 tablespoons	1½ pounds
Potato Chips	25	¾ to 1 ounce	1 to 1½ pounds

QUATRE-ÉPICES *(kä' truh e' pis)*—The name given to a French spice and herb mixture. Literally, it means four spices; however, more spices are usually used.

QUENELLE *(kuh nel')*—Various-sized meat, poultry, or seafood dumplings popular in French cookery. The forcemeat, which is a very finely ground mixture, is formed into balls or ovals, poached, and then used as a garnish or served with a sauce.

QUICHE *(kēsh)*—An open-faced tart of French origin that is filled with an unsweetened custard filling and flavored with bacon, cheese, meat, or seafood. The well-known Quiche Lorraine contains bacon and sometimes cheese, onion, or seafood. This particular tart originated in the Lorraine province of France.

Quiches are baked in a pie plate or a special quiche pan with fluted, straight sides. The large, custard tarts are impressively served as a main dish, while miniature versions are found on the appetizer tray. (See also *French Cookery.*)

Quiche Lorraine

 1 9-inch *unbaked* pastry shell
  (See *Pastry*)
 8 slices bacon, diced
 8 ounces natural Swiss cheese,
  shredded (2 cups)

   • • •

 1 tablespoon all-purpose flour
 ½ teaspoon salt
  Dash ground nutmeg
 3 beaten eggs
 1½ cup milk

Bake unpricked pastry shell at 450° only 5 minutes. Remove shell from oven. Reduce oven temperature to 325°.

Cook bacon till crisp; drain and crumble. Reserving 2 tablespoons crumbled bacon, place remaining bacon in partially baked pastry shell. Add shredded cheese. Combine flour, salt, nutmeg, eggs, and milk; pour over bacon and cheese in pastry shell. Trim with reserved bacon. Bake at 325° till knife inserted just off-center comes out clean, about 35 to 40 minutes. Let cool 10 minutes before serving. Serves 6.

Shrimp Quiche

Toss together 4 ounces process Swiss cheese, shredded (1 cup); 4 ounces Gruyère cheese, shredded; and 1 tablespoon all-purpose flour. Beat together 3 eggs, 1 cup light cream, ½ teaspoon prepared mustard, ¼ teaspoon salt, ¼ teaspoon Worcestershire sauce, dash bottled hot pepper sauce, and dash pepper. Prepare pastry for 1-crust 9-inch pie (See *Pastry*). Line 6 individual bakers with pastry. Divide about ¾ of the cheese mixture between the pastry-lined bakers. Add one 10-ounce package frozen, peeled, and cleaned shrimp, thawed and diced (about 1 cup). Add remaining cheese mixture. Pour into egg mixture.

Bake at 400° till knife inserted just off-center comes out clean, about 30 minutes. If desired, garnish with whole cooked shrimp and parsley. Makes 6 servings.

QUICK BREAD—Any one of several breads and breadlike foods that are made with quick-acting leavening, such as baking powder, baking soda, and steam. Biscuits, muffins, nut and fruit loaves, coffee cakes, pancakes, crêpes, fritters, and waffles fall into this group of quick-to-prepare breads. (See also *Breads.*)

Raisin-Nut Bread

In saucepan combine 1 cup raisins and 1 cup water; bring to boiling. Remove from heat; cool the mixture to room temperature.

Mix together 1 beaten egg, ¾ cup sugar, and ½ teaspoon vanilla; stir in raisin mixture. Sift together 1½ cups sifted all-purpose flour, 1 teaspoon baking powder, ¼ teaspoon baking soda, and ¼ teaspoon salt. Add to egg-raisin mixture, beating well. Stir in ¼ cup chopped walnuts. Pour into 2 greased and floured 16-ounce fruit cans. Bake at 350° till the bread tests done, about 50 to 60 minutes.

Variation of a classic

Serve Shrimp Quiche with refreshing iced →
tea and a green salad tossed with hearts of palm at an elegant luncheon for six.

QUICK COOKERY

Creative ways to quicker meals and menu plans for the busy, modern homemaker.

Homemakers have been searching for ways to speed up meal preparation ever since the first cavewoman decided that she was spending too much time slaving over a hot fire. Through the years many timesaving methods and products have been developed. However, the modern homemaker must evaluate expense in terms of money and time when using them. In the following recipes the cost of the food is more, but the meal is prepared in a jiffy.

Chicken and Biscuit Pie

>   1   15¼-ounce can chicken in gravy
>   1   10½-ounce can condensed cream
>   of chicken soup
>   1   tablespoon instant minced onion
>   ½   teaspoon dried rosemary leaves,
>   crushed
>   1   8-ounce can peas, drained
>   1   3-ounce can sliced
>   mushrooms, drained
>   1   5-ounce can boned chicken,
>   diced
>   1   tube refrigerated biscuits
>   (10 biscuits)

Mix first 4 ingredients. Add peas, mushrooms, and chicken. Heat slowly, stirring occasionally, till boiling. Turn into 2-quart casserole. Snip each biscuit in 3 wedges; arrange, points up, atop *hot* chicken mixture. Bake at 450° till biscuits are done, 15 minutes. Serves 5.

Quick dinner with a German accent

← Prove that jiffy meals can be interesting. Feature Skillet Potato Salad with bologna rings and deviled eggs in a supper menu.

In Chicken and Biscuit Pie many convenience foods are used—canned chicken, canned gravy, instant onion, and refrigerated biscuits. If you stewed a chicken, made your own soup, chopped the onion, and made biscuits, the cost of the recipe would be much lower. However, if you do not have the time to do all of this work yourself, the savings in time are well worth the extra cost. It all depends on what you have more of—time or money.

Ways to save time

Basically, there are three things that make quick cookery possible—convenience food products, timesaving equipment, and efficient work habits.

Convenience food products: Today's homemakers have at their disposal a boundless array of canned, boxed, and frozen foods. Some of these products are handy ingredients to use in recipes; others are complete dishes in themselves. These complete dishes can also form the bases for an entirely different but still quick dish when other ingredients are added.

There are many reasons why you might want to have convenience foods on hand. They are good to have for emergency meals. They are easy to fix, so novice cooks can prepare meals easily and children can assist their mothers in the kitchen. They are helpful to the homemaker who is employed outside of the home or one who spends a great deal of time with either club or charity work. For instance, the busy woman can put a hot meal before her family in very little time by using convenience products to make Skillet Potato Salad to serve as the main dish for supper or Orange-Nut Ring for breakfast.

Skillet Potato Salad

5 slices bacon
1 10½-ounce can condensed cream
    of celery soup
2 tablespoons sweet pickle relish
1 tablespoon instant minced onion
2 tablespoons vinegar
½ teaspoon salt
1 tablespoon chopped canned
    pimiento
2 16-ounce cans sliced potatoes,
    drained
1 14-ounce bologna ring

Fry bacon till crisp; remove from skillet. Drain and crumble. Drain off bacon drippings and return 1 tablespoon to skillet. Blend in soup, relish, onion, vinegar, salt, and pimiento. Cook and stir till mixture comes to boiling.

Gently stir in sliced potatoes and all *but* 1 tablespoon crumbled bacon. Score bologna ring and lay on top of salad in skillet. Simmer, covered, till bologna is heated through, 10 minutes. Sprinkle remaining bacon over top. Garnish with snipped parsley, if desired. Serves 6.

Orange-Nut Ring

2 packages refrigerated orange or
    cinnamon Danish rolls with
    icing (16 rolls)
¼ cup chopped pecans

Separate rolls and arrange 1 package (8 rolls), flat side down, around the bottom of *ungreased* 6½-cup ring mold. Stagger the remaining package of rolls on top of the first layer, covering the seams of the rolls on bottom layer.

Bake at 375° for 20 to 25 minutes. Invert on serving plate while it is still warm. Spread top and sides with frosting included in packages. Decorate with nuts. Serve warm. Serves 8.

Timesaving equipment: Modern equipment is largely responsible for making quick cookery possible. The electric mixer, one of the first modern appliances, is often taken for granted. It shouldn't be. It saves you time and energy. It will speed up the thorough mixing so necessary for making a cake from a mix or standard recipe.

The electric blender, too, has many uses. Use it properly and you will speed up your techniques. Blenders chop, grate, purée, and blend in a matter of seconds.

Strawberry-Lemonade Slush

A blender-made thirst quencher—

2 cups strawberries
1 cup sugar
3 cups water
1 cup lemon juice
    Few drops red food coloring
    Crushed ice
    Strawberry and lemon slices

Purée strawberries in blender container. Combine sugar, *1 cup* water, and lemon juice; stir till sugar is dissolved. Add remaining water, the puréed berries, and food coloring. Serve over crushed ice with strawberry and lemon slice floaters. Makes 6 cups.

There are many other appliances that save you time and effort. For example, pressure pans cook foods in approximately a third of the regular time; electric knives slice quickly with little effort; electric skillets and griddles control the heat to eliminate pot-watching, and automatic timers on ovens and range outlets begin and stop the cooking automatically. Toasters, coffee makers, can openers, and microwave ovens are helpers, too.

Efficient work habits: One of the least expensive factors in quick cookery is your work habits. You save time and energy by constantly evaluating and improving. When you go to the refrigerator, get several items at one time instead of making several trips. Also line up foods when slicing so you can slice several with each stroke.

A great way to start the day

For a speedy meal, serve Canadian-style → bacon, Berry-Cereal Parfaits (see *Cereal* for recipe), and an Orange-Nut Ring.

Timesaving tips

• Eliminate wiping up crumbs. Crush cookies and crackers in a plastic bag with a rolling pin if you do not have a blender.
• Shake cookies in a bag to coat with sugar, as when coating meats with crumbs. This makes fast work of rolling hot cookies.
• Plan an entire meal that bakes in the oven. You will be free to do other things while dinner bakes without any watching.
• Make salad dressing in large quantities. Shake, store, and serve in the same bottle.
• Set the table the night before for a quick breakfast or for a large dinner party.
• Measure dry ingredients and set out utensils early when you have some extra time.
• Reduce dishwashing and cluttered work areas by washing up as you work and by mixing, baking, and serving in one dish.

Finding new ways of doing things will also speed up your work a great deal. Try using convenience products available on the market and ideas in cookbooks, magazines, or newspapers to see if they work well for you. Move your timesaving appliances to a handy place, and learn to use them to the fullest advantage.

Double up on your tasks to save time later on. When shredding cheese, make some extra to freeze for another time. Make two casseroles or dessert recipes as long as all the ingredients are out, and put the second one in the freezer for a quick meal later in the month.

Dovetail your jobs when cooking a meal. Overlap recipe steps so you are not waiting for one thing to finish before you begin another. Do all the chopping or measuring for the whole meal at the same time.

Quick menus

The art of quick cookery involves careful planning and carrying out the plan well. In the following menus for breakfasts, lunches, and dinners, note the suggestions for preparing these carefully selected menus in a minimum of time and with as little wasted effort as possible.

Breakfast: The morning meal is one of the most vital meals of the day, but unfortunately it is too often neglected. You can serve tasty breakfasts in a jiffy by incorporating quick-cooking foods, such as cereals, in the breakfast menus.

Butterscotch Oatmeal

Round out the menu with chilled apple juice, toast, and brown-and-serve sausage—

   1 beaten egg
1¾ cups milk
  ½ cup brown sugar
   1 cup quick-cooking rolled oats
   2 tablespoons butter or margarine

In saucepan combine beaten egg, milk, and brown sugar. Cook and stir over medium heat till slightly thickened, about 5 minutes. Stir in oats; cook just till mixture begins to bubble, 3 minutes. (For creamier texture add oatmeal to *uncooked* egg mixture; cook and stir over medium heat till thickened, 8 to 10 minutes.) Add butter; cover and remove from heat. Let stand a few minutes, then stir to blend. Serve with light cream, if desired. Serves 2 or 3.

Other convenience products for breakfast include canned, fresh, and frozen berries, fruits, and juices. They are good in combinations as well as by themselves. There are also precooked sausages, dehydrated hashbrowns, and packaged, frozen refrigerated breads that take a minimum of work. Refrigerated rolls and biscuits are the bases of quick coffee cakes, such as Quick Apple Pinwheel and Orange-Nut Ring.

Another way to make a quick breakfast is to combine the main foods into one dish such as a soup and to do some of the work the evening before. In the following menu, dice the ham and boil the egg the day before. Also, place a package of frozen strawberries in the refrigerator to thaw and a can of pineapple in the refrigerator to chill. In the morning, start the coffee and make the ham soup first. While the soup is heating, drain the pineapple and mix it with icy strawberries. Make the toast and everything is ready to serve.

Cream of Ham Soup

  2 tablespoons butter or margarine
  2 tablespoons all-purpose flour
  ¼ teaspoon salt
    Dash white pepper
2½ cups milk
  1 cup diced fully cooked ham
  1 hard-cooked egg, finely chopped
    Toasted round oat cereal

In saucepan melt the butter. Blend in flour, salt, and pepper. Add milk all at once. Cook and stir till thickened and bubbly. Add ham and chopped egg; heat through. Top each serving with oat cereal. Makes 3 or 4 servings.

Lunch: Quick midday meals usually feature soups, sandwiches, or leftovers. Include relishes, chips, milk, cookies, fruit, and other prepared items to fill out the menu and to keep the work simple.

    Sandwiches are a favorite that please the cook and the diners. You can simplify the preparation by letting everyone stack his own or by grilling hot sandwiches at the table on a portable appliance. To spark interest, add something different to old standards. For instance, Avocado Open-Facers combine avocado with the popular bacon, lettuce, and tomato sandwich.

Variation of bacon-lettuce-tomato

Avocado Open-Facers make a colorful lunch. Just add crisp chips, relishes, iced tea, and fruit for a quick, nourishing menu.

Hasten the setting of gelatin by placing the bowl in a larger bowl of ice and water till partially set. Then, fold in fruit.

Avocado Open-Facers

    3 tablespoons mayonnaise or salad
        dressing
    1 tablespoon lemon juice
    4 slices whole wheat bread,
        toasted
    1 avocado, peeled and sliced
        Leaf lettuce
    1 tomato, thinly sliced
        Salt and pepper
    8 slices bacon, crisp-cooked and
        drained
        Thousand Island salad dressing

Combine mayonnaise and *half* the lemon juice; spread on one side of each slice toast. Brush avocado with remaining lemon juice. Place leaf lettuce, tomato slices, and avocado slices on toast. Sprinkle with salt and pepper. Crisscross 2 bacon slices atop each. Spoon on Thousand Island dressing. Garnish plate with relishes, if desired. Makes 4 sandwiches.

Soup is another welcome lunch. You can use canned or packaged soups and add zest with seasonings, or make classics quickly with convenience products. Quick Clam Chowder, for example, made with frozen and canned products, is a hearty lunch. Make a cake ahead so that everything is ready when the gang arrives.

Quick Clam Chowder

    1 7½-ounce can minced clams
    ¼ cup chopped celery
    1 teaspoon instant minced onion
    1 tablespoon butter or margarine
    1 8-ounce package frozen green peas
        and potatoes with cream sauce
    1 13¾-ounce can condensed
        chicken broth
    1 6-ounce can evaporated milk
    ¼ teaspoon dried thyme leaves,
        crushed
        Dash salt
        Dash pepper

Drain clams, reserving liquid. Cook celery and onion in butter till tender but not brown. Stir in next 6 ingredients and clam liquid. Cook and stir till mixture is boiling. Reduce heat; cover and simmer 5 minutes. Stir in clams; heat to boiling. Garnish the chowder with paprika, if desired. Makes 4 to 6 servings.

Pink and White Marble Cake

    1 package angel cake mix
        Red food coloring
    ¼ teaspoon peppermint extract
    1 package fluffy white frosting
        mix

Prepare cake mix according to package directions. Tint a third of batter pink with few drops food coloring; add extract. Spoon red and white batter alternately into *ungreased* 10-inch tube pan. Bake as directed. Invert; cool. Prepare frosting according to package directions; tint pink. Frost cooled cake.

MENU

QUICK WEEKEND LUNCH
Quick Clam Chowder
Crackers
Pink and White Marble Cake
Milk   *Tea*

MENU

MEXICAN LUNCH

Enchilada Casserole

Celery Sticks   Carrot Sticks

Tortilla Chips

Milk   Tea

Lunch menus planned around casseroles, such an Enchilada Casserole, are quick because all the foods cook together. When preparing Mexican Lunch, make the casserole and put it in to bake. Clean the carrots and celery, set the table, fill the glasses, and you'll have a few minutes to spare before serving lunch.

Enchilada Casserole

1 6-ounce package corn chips
8 ounces sharp process American
     cheese, shredded (2 cups)
1 15-ounce can chili with beans
1 15-ounce can enchilada sauce
1 8-ounce can tomato sauce
1 tablespoon instant minced onion
1 cup dairy sour cream

Reserve 1 cup chips. Combine remaining chips with 1½ *cups* cheese, chili with beans, enchilada sauce, tomato sauce, and instant onion. Pour into 11x7x1½-inch baking pan. Bake, uncovered, at 375° till hot, 30 minutes. Spread top of mixture with sour cream. Sprinkle with remaining cheese. Circle reserved chips around edge. Bake 5 minutes. Makes 6 servings.

Dinner: The largest meal of the day requires more dishes and, therefore, more planning in order to be quick. Canned and frozen meats and vegetables are outstanding time-savers. These convenience products make delicious meals when you use imaginative sauces and seasonings to dress them up. The following vegetable recipes illustrate how you can add interest.

Green Beans Plus

1 cup sliced celery
2 tablespoons butter or margarine
1 teaspoon sugar
2 16-ounce cans cut green beans

Cook celery in butter till crisp-tender; add sugar. Heat beans; drain. Toss with celery mixture. Season with salt and pepper. Serves 6 to 8.

Shrimp-Almond Sauce

1 3-ounce package cream cheese
     with chives
¼ cup milk
1 10-ounce can frozen condensed
     cream of shrimp soup
2 teaspoons lemon juice
2 tablespoon sliced almonds

Blend cheese and milk. Add soup. Heat and stir till hot. Add juice. Pour over hot vegetables. Toast nuts; sprinkle over sauce. Makes 1½ cups.

Gourmet vegetable dishes can be quick. Cook frozen broccoli spears or cauliflower while making a Shrimp-Almond Sauce.

MENU
OVEN MEAL
Luncheon Meat Dinner

Men's Favorite Salad

Bread   *Butter*

Busy-Day Cake

Caramel Sundae Topping

Coffee   *Milk*

Another way to make dinner quickly is to prepare oven meals. Arrange the menu, such as the following one so that everything bakes together at one temperature.

Luncheon Meat Dinner

  2 12-ounce cans luncheon meat
½ cup orange marmalade
  1 18-ounce can sweet potatoes, drained
  1 8½-ounce can sliced pineapple, halved
¼ cup butter or margarine, melted

Slice each piece of meat crosswise 3 times, slicing ¾ *of the way through*. Spread with marmalade. Place in an 11¾x7½x1¾-inch baking dish. Arrange potatoes around meat. Brush pineapple with butter. Insert in cuts in meat. Add remaining slices to dish with potatoes. Drizzle remaining butter over potatoes. Bake at 375° till browned, about 30 minutes. Baste the meat often. Makes 6 to 8 servings.

Men's Favorite Salad

  5 cups torn lettuce
  5 cups torn romaine
⅓ cup Italian salad dressing
  1 3½-ounce can French-fried onions
     Tomato wedges

Combine lettuce and romaine; add dressing and toss. Heat onions at 375° a few minutes to crisp. Toss warm onions gently with salad. Garnish with tomato. Serve at once. Serves 6.

Busy-Day Cake

⅓ cup shortening
1¾ cups sifted cake flour
¾ cup sugar
2½ teaspoons baking powder
½ teaspoon salt
 1 egg
¾ cup milk
1½ teaspoons vanilla

Place shortening in mixing bowl. Sift in dry ingredients. Add egg and *half* the milk; mix till flour is moistened. Beat 2 minutes at medium speed on electric mixer. Add remaining milk and vanilla; beat 2 minutes longer. Bake in greased and floured 9x9x2-inch baking pan at 375° till done, about 25 minutes.

Creamy Pumpkin-Whip Pie

  1 6½-ounce package graham cracker crust mix
  1 3¾-ounce package vanilla whipped dessert mix
  1 cup cold milk
  1 cup canned pumpkin
1½ teaspoons pumpkin pie spice
  1 2-ounce package dessert topping mix
½ teaspoon vanilla

Prepare crust mix according to directions for 9-inch pie. Whip dessert mix with ½ *cup* cold milk. Add pumpkin and spice; beat. Prepare topping with remaining milk and vanilla. Fold into pumpkin. Pour into crust. Chill.

MENU
JIFFY COMPANY DINNER
Fruit Juice Appetizer

Sweet-Sour Meatballs

Hot Rice   *Tomato Slices*

Creamy Pumpkin-Whip Pie

or Butterscotch Torte Supreme

Tea

Sweet-Sour Meatballs

    1 8¾-ounce can pineapple tidbits
    ¼ cup brown sugar
    2 tablespoons cornstarch
    ½ cup water
    ¼ cup cider vinegar
    1 teaspoon soy sauce
    1 5-ounce can water chestnuts
    1 16-ounce can meatballs in gravy
    1 green pepper, cut in strips

Drain pineapple, reserving syrup. In medium saucepan combine brown sugar and cornstarch. Blend in reserved syrup, water, vinegar, and soy sauce. Cook and stir over low heat till thickened and bubbly. Drain and thinly slice water chestnuts. Stir chestnuts, meatballs in gravy, green pepper, and pineapple into sauce mixture. Heat to boiling. Makes 4 servings.

Butterscotch Torte Supreme

    1 package 2-layer-size yellow
        cake mix
    1 3¾- or 4-ounce package *regular*
        butterscotch pudding mix
    1 8-ounce package pitted dates,
        snipped (1¼ cups)
        Dash salt
    ½ cup chopped walnuts
    2 tablespoons butter or margarine
                • • •
    1 package fluffy white frosting mix

Prepare cake mix according to package directions; bake in two 9-inch round pans. Cool thoroughly. Cut layers in half.

Meanwhile, prepare pudding according to directions, *using only 1½ cups milk and adding dates and salt.* When done, remove from heat; add nuts and butter. Place waxed paper directly on surface; cool to room temperature.

Spread pudding between cake layers and over top. Prepare frosting mix according to package directions. Spread on sides and add 1½-inch border of frosting on top of cake. Store any leftover cake in the refrigerator.

QUINCE *(kwins)* — A hard, yellow fruit resembling an apple or pear. Quinces have long been grown and enjoyed as food.

Identify quince by its golden yellow color and applelike shape. It has an acid-bitter pulp and seeds throughout the fruit.

At one time, quinces were considered sacred to the Goddess of Love and were given as a token of love. Luckily for today's women, fate interceded and replaced it with the diamond as an engagement symbol.

Quinces are usually grown locally and are available during the fall months. Ripe, desirable ones are pale yellow, firm, and free from blemishes. Quinces bruise quite easily, so be sure to handle them gently. Store them in a cool, dry place and they will keep very well.

When you are ready to use quinces, peel and core them and remove the hard seeds. Quinces must be cooked before eating or they will not be easily digested. You can make them into tart jellies, jams, and preserves. Or try stewing them for a dessert, a sauce, or an accompaniment to main dishes. One 3½-ounce quince contains 57 calories before it is cooked. It also contributes B vitamins, vitamin C, and carbohydrates to the diet. (See also *Fruit.*)

QUININE WATER *(kwī′ nīn)*—A carbonated beverage also called tonic or tonic water. Quinine water is made with the bitter-flavored quinine, lemon, and lime.

Quinine water mixes well with liquor and is used in many tall drinks. Gin and vodka are mixed with quinine water and lime juice for the popular summertime drink, gin and tonic or vodka and tonic. Thoroughly chilling the quinine water before making these drinks helps to keep the drinks cool and refreshing.

R

RABBIT—1. A long-eared animal related to the hare. **2.** Another name for Welsh Rabbit.

If you have a hunter in the family, chances are he will be bringing rabbit home since rabbit is the game most hunted in the United States. The entrails should be removed and the blood drained right after the animals are shot. The skin should be removed as soon as possible. Other than this, wild ones are prepared like the domestic rabbits you buy.

Plan to use fresh rabbit within two days. Cook rabbit as you would chicken, substituting it in your favorite poultry recipe if you like. Young rabbits are suitable to panfry, broil, and roast.

Fried Rabbit

- ¼ cup all-purpose flour
- ¾ teaspoon salt
  Dash pepper
- 1 1- to 1½-pound ready-to-cook young rabbit, cut up
- 2 tablespoons shortening

Combine flour, salt, and pepper. Coat rabbit with the flour mixture. In a skillet brown the meat slowly in hot shortening. Reduce heat; add 2 or 3 tablespoons water. Cover; simmer till tender, about 30 minutes, adding more water if necessary. Makes 2 servings.

Older rabbits should be braised or stewed, as in the famous hasenpfeffer and jugged hare. Rabbits are often soaked in brine, wine, or vinegar before cooking.

A 3½-ounce serving of raw wild rabbit contains 124 calories, while raw domestic rabbit has 159 calories. (See also *Game*.)

RACCOON—A small animal with a bushy, ringed tail. Raccoons, also called coons, are about 2½ to 3 feet long and weigh from 7 to 12 pounds. They were a source of food in pioneer days, and today they are hunted for food and sport during fall and winter.

The raccoon's dark flesh is tender and flavorful when prepared properly. Be sure to remove all the fat and the scent glands (small, round kernels). Raccoon is cooked like rabbit. Young ones are suitable for roasting whole; older raccoons are better braised and stewed. (See also *Game*.)

RACK OF LAMB—Another name for standing rib roast of lamb. (see also *Lamb*.)

RACLETTE *(rak let')*—A Swiss cheese dish that is related to fondue. As the cheese is melted, the softened parts are scraped off and eaten with bread or potatoes.

RADISH—An edible root vegetable belonging to the mustard family. The word is derived from the Latin word *radi* meaning root.

Although there is a distinct possibility that the radish originated in eastern Asia, varying forms of this vegetable have been cultivated for so many years that its origin is obscure. The Egyptians are known to have eaten radishes years before the pyramids were built, and the Greeks and Romans enjoyed them, too. These radishes, however, were much larger in size and were eaten in quantities like Americans eat corn and beans.

Various types of radishes are grown today—small and large; round and oblong; red, white, black, and purple. The small, round, red and the long, white icicle varieties are the most common at supermarkets. The large, white daikon or oriental radish, when available in the United States, is best known in its pickled form.

Nutritional value: Radishes contribute taste pleasure with their peppery flavor and crisp texture, but their nutritional offering is limited. They are quite low in calories (10 small radishes provide only 17 calories), and they contain vitamin C and other vitamins and minerals.

How to select and store: Radishes are marketed throughout the year, with the most plentiful supply appearing between May and July. Choose medium-sized radishes that are crisp and firm to the touch. Radishes that yield to pressure are more than likely overgrown, stale, and pithy. Avoid those that have cuts or any evidence of damage, too. Yellowed or decayed tops do not necessarily indicate poor quality.

At home, store radishes tightly covered in the refrigerator crisper. They will stay fresh in this way for about one week.

How to prepare and use: Before using radishes, wash them and remove the tops and root ends. Leave them whole for a relish tray or garnish. Slice them for use in salads, sandwiches, or vegetable dishes.

Although radishes are most often thought of as a relish food in this country, they are enjoyed in many different ways around the globe. In France, they are sliced, then buttered and salted. Mideastern cooks steam or boil the radish greens only. In Southeast Asia, one type of radish

is highly valued for its fleshy, seed pots, which are eaten raw or pickled. In China and Japan, the daikon is commonly prepared this way. (See also *Vegetable.*)

Panama Radish Salad

1½ cups sliced radishes
1 cup finely diced tomato
¼ cup thinly sliced onion rings
2 tablespoons salad oil
2 tablespoons lemon juice
2 teaspoons snipped parsley
½ teaspoon salt
⅛ teaspoon garlic salt
⅛ teaspoon black pepper

Combine radishes, tomato, and onion rings. In screw-top jar shake together remaining ingredients. Pour over radish mixture; toss. Chill for about 1 hour. Makes 4 to 5 servings.

RAGOUT *(ra gōō')*—A highly seasoned French stew. Ragout is made with fish, meat, or poultry. The meat is browned and cooked like a typical stew. Vegetables may or may not be included in the stew.

French Ragout

1½ cups sliced onion
3 tablespoons butter or margarine
1 beef bouillon cube
1½ cups water
2 cups cubed cooked beef
¾ cup leftover *or* canned gravy
1 lemon slice
1½ cups diced peeled potatoes
1½ cups sliced carrots
12 dried pitted prunes
¾ teaspoon salt
¼ cup cold water
1 tablespoon cornstarch

Cook onion in butter just till tender. Add remaining ingredients *except* cornstarch. Bring to a boil. Simmer, covered, for about 25 minutes. Blend cold water with the cornstarch. Stir into the beef mixture. Bring to a boil, stirring constantly. Simmer the mixture, uncovered, 5 minutes longer. Makes 4 servings.

RAINBOW TROUT—A variety of fresh-water trout that is recognizable by its colorful markings—a pink stripe running the entire length of the body, and many dark spots on the fins, body, and head. The rainbow trout is a popular game fish and is found across the United States and in Canada. Some rainbow trout, known as steel-heads, migrate to the ocean and then return to a freshwater stream.

The average weight of a rainbow trout is between two and eight pounds. The rainbow is a fat fish—a 3½-ounce portion of uncooked flesh equals 195 calories. It is a good source of high-quality protein and also contains the B vitamins.

Prepare rainbow trout by frying, baking, broiling, or poaching. (See also *Trout*.)

RAISIN—A grape that has been dried by natural or artificial methods. Not all grapes make good raisins, just as not all apples cook well. Only varieties that ripen to at least 18 percent sugar content and that have outstanding flavor, texture, and cooking characteristics when dried are used for raisins. Four pounds of fresh grapes will yield one pound of raisins.

More than likely, raisins are one of the oldest processed foods known to man. Prehistoric murals illustrate the very early use of raisins for jewelry and decoration, and religious and magical powers were attributed to these fruits, too.

There were also many functional uses for raisins. As food, they were often included in the menu at feasts of the Roman emperor Nero. Monetarily, they were used by the Israelites as tax payments to King David, and in Rome the value of a slave was indicated by the number of raisins placed into a narrow-necked vessel called an amphor. As medicine, they were suggested for the psychological relief of anger and sorrow by Egyptian doctors, and for the cure of dysentery, coughs, and certain poisons by Roman physicians.

Raisins were being produced long before the Christian Era. Four thousand years ago Armenia was the center of raisin production, and it remained so for 1,500 years. Greece and Spain provided only a small amount of the total poundage. Today, production is centered in California.

The early Spanish missionaries were largely responsible for the production of raisins in America. As they moved into California, they planted vineyards as sources for the missions' sacramental wines. By the 1850s, both the Sacramento and San Joaquin valleys were important production areas. Today, San Joaquin is the world's largest raisin-producing center.

Unforeseen weather conditions were responsible for changing the emphasis from grapes to raisins in the San Joaquin Valley. In 1873, summer and fall were so hot and dry that the grapes dried on the vines before they could be picked. In an effort to reduce the financial loss, one enterprising grower shipped the dried grapes to a grocer friend in San Francisco. A ship from Peru that had docked at the bay inspired the grocer to market the raisins as "Peruvian delicacies." The promotion was such a success that the foundations for the raisin industry were soon begun.

Nutritional value: Raisins contain the nutritive value of grapes in a concentrated form. The high sugar content is a good source of quick energy. One and one-half tablespoons of raisins contain 40 calories; 1 cup contains 408 calories. Raisins have all of the vitamins and minerals needed to convert raisin sugar to energy without borrowing from body stores.

Types of raisins: Raisins are often given the name of the grape variety from which they come, such as Muscat and Thompson Seedless. Dried Muscats were the first raisins marketed in the United States, but they are scarcely available now. Thompson Seedless have surpassed Muscats in availability. Zante currants (from the Black Corinthian grape variety) are also important.

Nearly all the California raisins marketed are of the Thompson Seedless variety. They are two forms of this variety, which vary in color and in the processing they undergo. Natural seedless raisins are medium brown in color and are naturally dried in the sun without any chemical additives. Golden raisins, with their rich yellow color, are dried artificially. The special drying procedures more nearly retain the natural color of the white grapes.

Small, dark Zante currants are a fourth the size of Thompson Seedless raisins. They are seedless and have a tart flavor. These currants are completely different from those used in currant jelly.

How raisins are produced: Practically all of the American-marketed raisins are produced and processed in the San Joaquin Valley of central California. In fact, almost half of the world's supply comes from a 100 mile area around Fresno. Except for golden raisins, the modern methods of raisin production still rely heavily on natural sun drying techniques without the use of chemical treatment.

In the traditional drying method, the grape bunches are picked from the vines in early September and placed on paper trays that lay between the vineyard rows. The grapes are arranged to give maximum sun exposure. For the next two weeks, hot dry weather is essential for the grapes to dry properly. The bunches are occasionally turned to ensure even dehydration.

When the moisture of the grapes has been reduced to about 15 percent, the raisins are rolled up in the paper trays for the journey to the grower's yard. There, they are put into sweat boxes or bins, which help to equalize the moisture in the raisins. The sweat boxes are stacked and tightly sealed in paper until they are sold.

The final stages of preparing the raisins for market are undertaken at the packing plant. The large grape stems are removed, and the raisins are carefully inspected, washed, and packed into an assortment of market-sized containers.

Golden raisins are produced by significantly different drying methods, but packing procedures remain essentially the same as for other raisins. After picking, the fresh grapes are transported immediately to the processing plant. There, they are treated in a special bath that readies the fruits for the drying operation. Next, the grapes go into ovens for sulfur dioxide treatment. This harmless chemical allows the grapes to retain their natural color. Prior to inspection and packing, the grapes are placed into the drying ovens where they must remain about 18 hours to achieve the proper moisture level.

How to select and store: Raisins are quite easy to purchase and store because of their versatility and stability.

You'll soon find the family congregating in the kitchen when the fragrant aroma of home-baked Raisin Loaves permeates the rest of the house. Serve the warm slices with butter pats.

Raisin varieties, in most cases, may be interchanged in recipes. The Thompson Seedless raisins are the most popular all-purpose variety. The brown one can be used for all dishes requiring raisins as well as for eating fresh as a snack food. Golden Thompson Seedless are used when special coloring is desired, such as in light fruitcakes and confections. Zante currants are traditionally used in hot cross buns and are ideal for rolls in which larger raisins would be less desirable.

The high sugar content of raisins acts as a natural preservative, thus, markedly improving their storage life as compared to the storage life of the fresh grapes. Store unopened boxes or bags of raisins at dry, room temperature conditions. Partially used boxes or bags of raisins should be sealed in a tightly covered container. Once opened, refrigeration prolongs freshness for extended storage.

How to prepare Plumping is a common cooking technique used in raisin preparation. For plumping, see the box below.

Contrary to popular belief, flouring (coating the fruit with flour) does not prevent raisins from sinking. The raisins sink because they are heavy with fruit sugar. Raisins must either be chopped or incorporated into a very stiff batter in order to keep them from sinking.

Ways to plump raisins

Plumped raisins are frequently used because of their added softness and moistness. Water is most often the liquid used, but fruit juice, coffee, brandy, or other liquid can be used to impart added flavor.

Plumping with water — Cover the raisins with very hot tap water and soak them 2 to 5 minutes, *or* cover the raisins with water in a saucepan and bring to boiling. Remove from heat; let stand 5 minutes.

Plumping with other liquid — Cover raisins with liquid. Soak raisins at room temperature for several hours or overnight.

How to knead and shape raisin bread

Knead raisin bread dough with heels of hands until the dough is smooth and satiny. This requires 8 to 10 minutes of kneading.

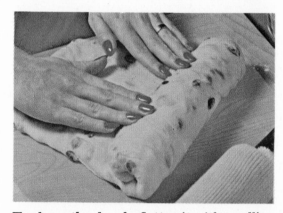

To shape the dough, flatten it with a rolling pin, making the width as long as the pan. Roll up dough from narrow end.

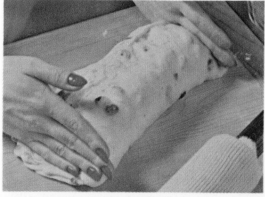

With edges of hands, seal ends of loaf. Fold the ends of dough under as the loaf is placed into the greased loaf pan.

How to use: Raisins possess worldwide popularity in a variety of different foods, such as side dishes, entrées, and desserts.

Raisin bread is popular in many different cuisines—in Ireland, it's called Irish soda bread; in Germany, raisin-filled *Stollen*. Americans love yeast-raised raisin bread drizzled with icing.

Raisin Loaves

In large mixer bowl combine 1 package active dry yeast and 2½ cups sifted all-purpose flour. In saucepan heat 2¼ cups milk, ⅓ cup sugar, ¼ cup shortening, and 2 teaspoons salt just till warm, stirring occasionally to melt shortening. Add warm liquid mixture to dry mixture.

Beat at low speed with electric mixer for ½ minute, scraping sides of bowl constantly. Beat 3 minutes at high speed. By hand, stir in 2 cups raisins and 3¼ to 3¾ cups sifted all-purpose flour to make moderately stiff dough. Turn out onto lightly floured surface; knead till smooth and satiny. Shape into a ball; place in lightly greased bowl, turning once. Cover; let dough rise in warm place till double.

Punch dough down. Cut in 2 portions.* Shape each into a smooth ball; cover and let rest for 10 minutes. Shape into loaves; place in 2 greased 9x5x3-inch loaf pans. Cover; let rise in warm place till double, 45 to 60 minutes. Bake at 400° for 35 minutes. While warm, drizzle with Confectioners' Icing, if desired (See *Confectioners' Sugar*). Makes 2 loaves.

*Or divide dough into 8 portions. Shape same as large loaves, placing in 4½x2¾x2¼-inch pans. Bake at 375° for 25 to 30 minutes.

Cinnamon Crescents

    1 package hot roll mix
    3 eggs
    6 tablespoons butter, softened
    ½ cup all-purpose flour
    2 tablespoons butter or margarine,
        melted
    1 cup raisins
    ½ cup sugar
    ½ cup chopped walnuts
    1 teaspoon ground cinnamon
        Confectioners' Icing (See
        Confectioners' Sugar)

Soften yeast from hot roll mix with ½ *cup water* following package directions. Beat eggs well in a large bowl. Add yeast, hot roll mix, and the 6 tablespoons softened butter or margarine. Blend the mixture well. Cover the dough; let it rise till double, about 1 hour.

Sprinkle the all-purpose flour on a board and knead it into the dough so that the dough is still very soft but not sticky. Divide dough in half. On a lightly floured surface roll *each half* of dough to a 12x10-inch rectangle. Brush with melted butter.

Combine raisins, sugar, nuts, and cinnamon; sprinkle *half* over each rectangle. Roll up in jelly-roll fashion, starting with long edge. Place, sealed sides down, on greased baking sheet, curving to form crescents and pinching ends to seal well. Cover and let rise till light, about ½ hour. Bake at 375° for 25 minutes. Frost with Confectioners' Icing. Top with additional nuts, if desired. Makes 2 crescents.

Australians, Indians, and Armenians as well as Americans like raisins in entrées and side dishes. In Australia, a well-seasoned stuffing with raisins is baked inside tender squabs. Raisins are a customary condiment for Indian curries. Raisins often are scattered throughout Armenian pilafs. Americans are well known for their baked ham with sweet raisin sauce and mayonnaise-dressed carrot-raisin salad.

Easy ways to chop and grind raisins

No matter which technique you choose, raisins are chopped and ground with stickless ease when you call on salad oil for help.

To chop raisins on a cutting board, coat each cup of raisins with about 1 teaspoon salad oil prior to chopping them.

For speed chopping, store the raisins in the freezer. At chopping time lightly oil blender container and blades with salad oil. Then chop ¼ to ½ cup raisins at a time.

To grind raisins, first oil the screw and blades of the food grinder.

Raisin Sauce

⅓ cup raisins
½ cup water
⅓ cup currant jelly
½ teaspoon grated orange peel
½ cup orange juice

. . .

2 tablespoons brown sugar
1 tablespoon cornstarch
Dash ground allspice
Dash salt

Combine raisins, water, jelly, orange peel, and orange juice in saucepan; bring to boiling. Combine brown sugar, cornstarch, allspice, and salt; stir into raisin mixture. Cook and stir till thickened and bubbly. Serve warm with fully cooked ham. Makes about 1½ cups.

Gingery Macaroni Salad

½ 7-ounce package elbow macaroni,
   cooked and drained
   (about 2 cups)
¼ cup light raisins
¼ cup chopped celery

. . .

½ cup mayonnaise or salad
   dressing
1 tablespoon chopped onion
1 teaspoon chopped candied ginger
¼ teaspoon salt
¼ teaspoon curry powder
Dash garlic salt
Dash pepper
2 tablespoons coarsely chopped
   peanuts

Combine macaroni, raisins, and celery. Blend together mayonnaise, onion, candied ginger, salt, curry powder, garlic salt, and pepper. Toss mayonnaise mixture lightly with macaroni mixture. Chill. Serve in lettuce cups; garnish with peanuts. Makes 4 to 6 servings.

Breakfast fanfare

← Alternate layers of coffee bread and moist raisin filling give nut- and icing-coated Cinnamon Crescents morningtime appeal.

Raisins are standouts in many international desserts, too. Italian fried cookies made with raisins are Christmas fare. In England, there's famed steamed puddings, once made with plums but now filled with currants and raisins. American versions of pies, cakes, puddings, and cookies, chock full of raisins, are unforgetably delicious, too. (See *Dried Fruit, Grape* for additional information.)

Raisin Pie

3 beaten eggs
1 cup sugar
½ teaspoon ground cinnamon
½ teaspoon ground nutmeg
¼ teaspoon salt
2½ tablespoons lemon juice
2 tablespoons butter or
   margarine, melted

. . .

1 cup raisins
⅓ cup broken walnuts
1 8-inch *unbaked* pastry shell
   (See *Pastry*)

Combine eggs, sugar, cinnamon, nutmeg, salt, lemon juice, and butter. Stir in raisins and the ⅓ cup broken walnuts. Pour the mixture into a pastry shell. Bake at 375° till filling is set in center, 35 to 40 minutes. Cool.

Old-Fashioned Raisin Bars

A spicy classic—

Combine 1 cup raisins and 1 cup water in a saucepan; bring to boiling. Remove the mixture from heat. Stir in ½ cup shortening *or* salad oil; cool mixture to lukewarm. Stir in 1 cup sugar and 1 slightly beaten egg.

Sift together 1¾ cups sifted all-purpose flour, 1 teaspoon baking soda, 1 teaspoon ground cinnamon, ½ teaspoon ground nutmeg, ½ teaspoon ground allspice, ¼ teaspoon salt, and ¼ teaspoon ground cloves; beat into raisin mixture. Stir in ½ cup chopped walnuts. Pour into a greased 15½x10½x1-inch baking pan. Bake at 375° for 12 minutes. When cool, cut in bars. Dust lightly with confectioners' sugar, or frost while warm. Makes about 4 dozen bars.

RAMEKIN *(ram' uh kin)*—**1.** A baked dish, usually based on cheese, that is prepared in individual serving dishes. **2.** A small baking container that holds an individual portion. Usually straight-sided, ramekins look like miniature soufflé dishes. The dishes are most often used for baking individual souffleś or casseroles.

RAMPION *(ram' pē uhn)*—A vegetable with a long, white root that resembles a large radish. Native to Europe, rampions are eaten raw or cooked. Europeans enjoy the roots and young leaves in salads.

RANCID—A word that describes the unpleasant aroma and flavor of fats and oils that have deteriorated or spoiled.

Although most common to foods high in fat, rancidity can occur theoretically in any food containing fat. Exposure to air, heat, light, and moisture hastens this reaction. Many of the commercial fats and oils contain antioxidants, which help retard this change. (See also *Fat*.)

RAPE—**1.** Grape stems and skins that remain after the juice has been pressed out in the winemaking process. The rape is sometimes used as a filter in vinegar production. **2.** A vegetable of the cabbage family that has edible leaves and a fleshy stem. Rape is little used for food in the United States, but abroad its warm, aromatic flavor is enjoyed in salads or as a cooked green. An edible oil is also extracted from rape seeds.

RAREBIT—Another name often used for the famous cheese dish, Welsh Rabbit. (See also *Welsh Rabbit*.)

RASPBERRY—A small, thimble-shaped fruit belonging to the rose family.

Whether red, black, purple, or amber, raspberries are, in the scientific sense, aggregate fruits rather than berries. According to the botanical definition, a berry consists of many seeds scattered throughout the pulp of a fruit, as in currants or grapes. Like all aggregate fruits, on the other hand, a raspberry is a cluster of fruits each of which contains one seed surrounded by pulp.

Early historical references to the existence of wild or cultivated raspberries are scattered throughout Europe. Raspberry seeds were excavated from both Swiss and Glastonbury lake dwellings, which existed during the Neolithic and Iron ages respectively. In the first century A.D. the Roman naturalist Pliny recorded the belief that raspberries came from Mt. Ida, Greece, an area of mythological importance. The first reference to raspberries in England appeared in an orchard book published in 1629 in which an entire chapter was devoted to red and white (amber-type) raspberries. By the 1800s, many good raspberry varieties were being cultivated in northern Europe.

By the time America was settled, Europeans were quite familiar with red raspberries. They found similar wild varieties growing in this country as well as the unfamiliar black raspberries, which were called "black caps." At first, only the wild berries were used, but as more territories were settled, raspberry cultivation became necessary to satisfy the demand. European plants were imported and for many years were more popular than the American raspberry varieties.

How raspberries are produced: Raspberry plants have a unique growth cycle. Although the roots of raspberry bushes are perennial, the thorny canes grow biennially. Fruits are produced during the second year of the cane's growth. Each year two-year-old canes are replaced by new canes. In addition to canes, the plants send out suckers. Both root cuttings and suckers are used to propagate new plants.

What are "black caps?"

Unfamiliar with the black raspberries that grew wild when America was settled, our forefathers nicknamed the berries "black caps" to distinguish them from blackberries. Like other raspberries, black raspberries separate from their stem caps and white cores when picked. Blackberries, on the other hand, do not separate from their cores and leave only the stem caps on the canes.

The colors purple (left front), black (right front), and red (rear) identify the three most popular raspberry varieties.

Raspberry cultivation requires careful training of the thorny canes to achieve greatest yield and to make the berries easily accessible for picking. The canes are either staked, trellised, or topped (tops pruned to promote branching). Pruning is carried out during spring or fall, depending on the raspberry variety.

Raspberry plants also need cool, moist climatic conditions. Because of these factors, the major raspberry-producing areas in the United States are in the north.

Nutritional value: Raspberries supply varying caloric, vitamin, and mineral values, depending on the variety. Black raspberries are higher in calories than red ones: 100 calories per cup of black raspberries; 70 calories per cup of red raspberries. Small amounts of the B vitamin thiamine, vitamin C, and minerals such as calcium, phosphorous, potassium, and iron are also present in raspberries.

Types of raspberries: The varieties presently important from a commercial standpoint have been adapted from the wild American species or from hybrid crossings of the American and European varieties. Red and black raspberries are the most popular. Purple (a cross of red and black) and amber ones are less well-known and are of less importance.

Raspberries have played a part in the hybridizing of new berry types, too. Loganberries are a cross between blackberries and red raspberries, and boysenberries are a blend of a raspberry, loganberry, and three blackberry varieties.

How to select: These very perishable fruit usually are marketed in the areas in which they are grown. Fresh raspberries are a summer luxury, but for year-round pleasure there are frozen and canned berries available in most supermarkets.

When selecting fresh raspberries, the appearance of the berries is of utmost importance. They should look clean, have bright, uniform color, and be plump. Avoid berries that are dirty, mashed, or wet, and those that have caps that are still fastened to the cores (underripe). Overripe raspberries are usually dull in color, soft, and leak excess juice.

How to store: Raspberries are one of the most delicate fresh fruits. Thus, they must be handled gently to ensure taste and appearance satisfaction when served.

The berries can be washed prior to storage if they are drained thoroughly on paper toweling. However, some homemakers prefer to wash the berries just before they are used. In either case, cover the dry berries lightly and refrigerate.

Because raspberries stay fresh for only a few days, use them as soon as possible after purchasing. Red raspberries are more perishable than are the black ones.

Freezing and canning can be employed when raspberries are in plenteous supply. The berries can be frozen unsweetened, mixed with sugar, or mixed with a sugar syrup, depending on whether they will be used for special dietary purposes, for cooking, or for eating right from the package. Canned preserves and jellies made from fresh raspberries provide fruit flavor during the off-seasons, too.

How to use: Raspberries are a family favorite whether served plain or fancy.

Raspberries are sandwiched between a crumb crust-meringue base and whipped dessert topping for Raspberry-Meringue Squares.

Fresh raspberries add color and flavor to morning cereal bowls and to midday salads. Raspberries with cream hit the spot as a morning appetizer or an evening dessert. Raspberries with or without other fruits take on gourmet dessert appeal simply with the addition of a flaming liqueur.

Red Raspberry Ring

Ice cream adds richness—

    1 10-ounce package frozen
        raspberries, thawed
    2 3-ounce packages red raspberry-
        flavored gelatin
    2 cups boiling water
    1 pint vanilla ice cream
    1 6-ounce can frozen pink lemonade
        concentrate, thawed (¾ cup)
    ¼ cup chopped pecans

Drain raspberries, reserving syrup. Dissolve gelatin in boiling water. Add ice cream by spoonfuls, stirring till melted. Stir in lemonade concentrate and the reserved syrup. Chill till partially set. Fold in raspberries and pecans. Turn into a 6½-cup ring mold. Chill till firm. Makes 8 to 10 servings.

Raspberry-Meringue Squares

    1½ cups vanilla wafer crumbs
     ¼ cup butter, melted
     2 tablespoons sugar
     4 egg whites
     ½ cup sugar
     1 pint red raspberries, slightly
         sweetened
     1 2-ounce package dessert topping
         mix
     1 tablespoon lemon juice

Combine crumbs, butter, and the 2 tablespoons sugar; mix well. Press firmly in bottom of 9x 9x2-inch baking pan. Beat egg whites till soft peaks form; gradually add the ½ cup sugar, beating to stiff peaks. Swirl meringue over crust; bake at 325° for 12 to 15 minutes. Cool.

Spread raspberries over meringue. Prepare dessert topping mix according to package directions; stir in lemon juice. Spread over berries; chill. Top with berries, if desired. Serves 9.

For more fanciful eating, use raspberries in your baking or in cold dishes. Let the aroma of freshly baked raspberry pie, cake, or shortbread permeate throughout the house. Versatile raspberry syrup or jam spruces up bread products as well as ice cream and sherbet. (See also *Berry*.)

Raspberry-Cream Cheese Coffee Cake

    1 3-ounce package cream cheese
    ¼ cup butter or margarine
    2 cups packaged biscuit mix
    ⅓ cup milk
    ½ cup raspberry preserves
    1 cup sifted confectioners' sugar
    1 to 2 tablespoons milk
    ½ teaspoon vanilla

Cut cream cheese and butter into biscuit mix till crumbly. Blend in the ⅓ cup milk. Turn onto floured surface; knead 8 to 10 strokes.

On waxed paper, roll dough to 12x8 inches. Turn onto greased baking sheet; remove paper. Spread preserves down center. Cut 2½x1-inch strips on long sides. Fold strips over filling. Bake at 425° for 12 to 15 minutes. Combine remaining ingredients; drizzle atop.

Red Raspberry Salad

    2 10-ounce packages frozen
        raspberries, thawed
    2 3-ounce packages red raspberry-
        flavored gelatin
    1 16-ounce can applesauce

Drain raspberries, reserving 1 cup syrup. Dissolve gelatin in 2 cups boiling water; stir in reserved syrup and applesauce. Chill till partially set; fold in raspberries. Pour into 6-cup ring mold; chill till firm. Serve 6 to 8.

RASPBERRY VINEGAR—A product made by steeping ripe raspberries in cider or in wine vinegar, then straining out the raspberries and sweetening the liquid to taste. It is used as a base for fruit beverages.

RATAFIA *(rat′ uh fe′ uh)*—**1.** General name for liqueurs flavored with fruit and/or fruit kernels. Ratafia once meant any liqueur drunk at the ratification of a treaty. **2.** An almond-flavored sweet biscuit.

RATATOUILLE *(râ tâ′ tuy)*—A well-seasoned vegetable stew or casserole that originated in Provence, France. Eggplant, squash, green pepper, tomatoes, garlic, and olive oil are traditional ingredients.

Eggplant Ratatouille

    2 medium onions, sliced (1½ cups)
    1 clove garlic, minced
    3 tablespoons olive oil
    2 small zucchini, cut in ½-inch
        slices
    2 tomatoes, peeled and diced
    1 small eggplant, chopped
    1 large green pepper, chopped
    1 bay leaf
    3 slices bacon

In Dutch oven cook onion and garlic in hot oil till tender but not brown. Add next 5 ingredients, 2 teaspoons salt, and dash pepper. Bring to boil; cover and simmer 30 minutes, stirring occasionally. Fry bacon till crisp; drain and crumble. Add to vegetables; simmer, uncovered, 10 minutes. Remove bay leaf. Serves 6.

RAVIGOTE BUTTER *(ra vē gôt′)*—Softened butter mixed with finely chopped green herbs, particularly tarragon, parsley, and chervil. Ravigote butter, sometimes called green butter, is usually served as an accompaniment to broiled meat.

RAVIGOTE SAUCE—**1.** A cold sauce made of mayonnaise, chopped chives, parsley, wine vinegar, and lemon juice, or an oil and vinegar mixture with hard-cooked egg yolks, mustard, and chopped herbs added. Cold ravigote sauce is usually served with seafood. **2.** A warm sauce made of wine, vinegar, green onion, white sauce, and crushed herbs. This piquant sauce is usually served with poultry, fish, or egg dishes.

Ravigote Sauce

Try this with broiled fish—

    ¼ cup snipped green onion
    1 tablespoon butter or margarine
    3 tablespoons dry white wine
    1 tablespoon vinegar
    1 tablespoon butter or margarine
    1 tablespoon all-purpose flour
    1 cup light cream
    ¼ teaspoon salt
    ¼ teaspoon dried tarragon leaves,
        crushed

In saucepan cook snipped green onion in 1 tablespoon butter or margarine till tender. Add dry white wine and vinegar. Simmer till liquid is reduced by half. Melt 1 tablespoon butter or margarine; blend in flour. Add light cream. Cook, stirring constantly, till mixture bubbles. Remove from heat; stir in salt and crushed tarragon. Return to low heat; *gradually* stir in onion mixture. Do not boil. Makes 1 cup.

RAVIOLI *(rav′ ē ō′ le, rä′ vē-)*—An Italian dish made of pasta dough cases filled with a meat or vegetable mixture. These Italian dumplings are boiled, then covered with a tomato sauce. Ravioli makes a delicious appetizer or a satisfying main dish. Although homemade ravioli is more authentic, canned or frozen ravioli can be used for those quick-to-prepare meals.

Chicken and Spinach-Filled Ravioli

A homemade dish with real Italian flavor that guests and family alike are sure to appreciate—

4 well-beaten eggs
¾ cup water
3¾ cups sifted all-purpose flour
1½ teaspoons salt

. . .

1 cup ground cooked chicken
1 8-ounce can spinach, well
    drained and chopped
3 tablespoons butter or margarine,
    melted
3 tablespoons grated Parmesan
    cheese
¼ teaspoon salt
⅛ teaspoon ground nutmeg
    Dash pepper
    Spicy Tomato Sauce

To make ravioli dough, combine well-beaten eggs and water in large bowl. Add *2 cups* flour and the 1½ teaspoons salt; beat well. Gradually stir in enough of remaining flour to make moderately stiff dough. Turn out on lightly floured surface and knead till smooth and elastic, about 8 to 10 minutes. Divide dough into two parts. Cover and let rest 10 minutes. Roll each part of dough out to a 16x12-inch rectangle. Cut each rectangle into 2-inch squares.

Combine ground chicken, chopped spinach, and melted butter or margarine. Stir in Parmesan cheese, ¼ teaspoon salt, ground nutmeg, and pepper. Place a teaspoon of filling on one two-inch square of dough. Moisten edges of dough with water and top with second square; seal well with tines of fork. Repeat with remaining filling and ravioli dough. Set aside to dry for 1 hour, turning once.

Cook ravioli in large kettle of rapidly boiling, salted water till tender, about 7 to 8 minutes. Rinse in cold water and drain well. Place in a 13½x8¾x1¾-inch baking dish. Pour Spicy Tomato Sauce over. Bake, covered, at 350° for 30 minutes. Makes 6 to 8 servings.

Spicy Tomato Sauce: In saucepan combine 1 cup water; one 15-ounce can tomato sauce (2 cups); one 7½-ounce can tomatoes (1 cup), cut up; 2 tablespoons snipped parsley; 2 teaspoons sugar; 1 teaspoon dried oregano leaves, crushed; and 1 teaspoon salt. Simmer, uncovered, for 30 minutes, stirring occasionally.

Inside-Out Ravioli

1 pound ground beef
½ cup chopped onion
1 clove garlic, minced
1 10-ounce package frozen chopped
    spinach
    Water
1 16-ounce can spaghetti sauce
    with mushrooms
1 8-ounce can tomato sauce
1 6-ounce can tomato paste
½ teaspoon salt
    Dash pepper

. . .

1 7-ounce package shell or elbow
    macaroni (2 cups), cooked
    and drained
4 ounces sharp process American
    cheese, shredded (1 cup)
½ cup soft bread crumbs
2 well-beaten eggs
¼ cup salad oil

In large skillet brown ground beef, chopped onion, and minced garlic. Cook chopped spinach according to package directions. Drain spinach, reserving liquid; add water to make 1 cup. Add spinach liquid, spaghetti sauce, tomato sauce, tomato paste, salt, and pepper to meat mixture. Simmer 10 minutes.

In mixing bowl combine drained spinach with cooked macaroni, shredded process American cheese, soft bread crumbs, well-beaten eggs, and salad oil; spread in 13x9x2-inch baking dish. Top with meat sauce. Bake at 350° for 30 minutes. Let stand 10 minutes before serving. Makes 8 to 10 servings.

REAMER *(rē′ muhr)*—A utensil that is used for extracting the juice from oranges, lemons, and limes. It consists of a shallow dish with a ribbed, inverted cone in the center. The juice is squeezed out of citrus fruit by inverting the fruit half over the center of the reamer and pressing the fruit against the cone. As the juice is extracted, it accumulates in the dish part of the reamer. In electric juicers of this type, the ribbed center revolves.

RÉCHAUFFÉ *(rā shō fā′)*—The French word for a reheated food or leftover.

RECIPE—A detailed guide to the preparation of ingredients and the cooking of a dish. A recipe includes the proportions of ingredients needed and the method in which these ingredients are to be put together. The yield is usually given, too.

To ensure success in the preparation and serving of a recipe, two preliminary steps are recommended. First, read through the entire recipe to get the complete picture of what the food is intended to be. Secondly, get all of the necessary ingredients out of storage to make sure that you have all that is called for.

If the dish is to be served at mealtime with several other foods, preparation will necessitate dovetailing work from one recipe to another. In this way, the dishes can be served at the planned time and in the proper sequence.

For the new cook, greatest success in preparing recipes is achieved by following recipe directions explicitly. In time, however, experienced homemakers become familiar with cooking principles and techniques, and thus, can take some liberties in making desired recipe alterations and ingredient substitutions.

RED BEAN—A dark red type of kidney bean. Although red beans are similar in flavor to the dark reddish purple kidney beans, their flavor is less intense. For this reason, they are frequently used to replace kidney beans when a milder flavor is desired. They are of great importance in Mexican cookery. (See also *Kidney Bean*.)

Red Bean Toss

1 16-ounce can red beans, drained
1 cup thinly sliced celery
⅓ cup chopped sweet pickle
¼ cup finely chopped onion
4 ounces sharp process American cheese, diced (1 cup)
½ teaspoon chili powder
½ teaspoon salt
½ teaspoon Worcestershire sauce
Few drops bottled hot pepper sauce
½ cup mayonnaise or salad dressing
1 cup coarsely crushed corn chips

Combine red beans, celery, sweet pickle, onion, and process American cheese. Blend chili powder, salt, Worcestershire sauce, and hot pepper sauce with mayonnaise; add this mixture to the bean mixture and toss lightly.

Spoon bean mixture into a 1-quart shallow baking dish; sprinkle with corn chips. Bake at 450° about 10 minutes. Garnish with green pepper rings, if desired. Makes 4 servings.

Bean and Cheese Patties

2 beaten eggs
¼ cup catsup
¼ cup finely crushed saltine crackers (7 crackers)
2 tablespoons chopped onion
2 teaspoons Worcestershire sauce
• • •
1 pound ground beef
1 tablespoon salad oil
1 10½-ounce can condensed cream of mushroom soup
• • •
1 16-ounce can red beans
⅓ cup chopped green pepper
4 ounces sharp process American cheese, shredded (1 cup)

Mix first 5 ingredients, ¼ teaspoon salt, and dash pepper. Add beef; mix well. Shape into 4 or 5 patties. Brown in hot oil; spoon soup over. Drain beans; sprinkle vegetables and cheese atop patties. Cook slowly, covered, 10 to 15 minutes. Makes 4 to 5 servings.

RED CABBAGE—A purplish red cabbage. The flavor and texture of red cabbage are identical to the green varieties. Thus, preparation and cooking techniques are the same for both types. To retain the color of the red cabbage during cooking, add an acidic food such as vinegar, lemon juice, or sliced apple to the cooking water. (See also *Cabbage*.)

RED CINNAMON CANDY—A small, round, red sugar candy flavored with cinnamon. Many people refer to them as "red hots." They may be eaten as a snack food or used in assorted fruit salad, dessert, and accompaniment recipes such as cinnamon apples.

Cinnamon-Apple Salad

Dissolve two 3-ounce packages lemon-flavored gelatin and ½ cup red cinnamon candies in 3 cups boiling water. Stir in 2 cups unsweetened applesauce, 1 tablespoon lemon juice, and dash salt. Chill till partially set. Add ½ cup broken walnuts. Pour into an 8x8x2-inch pan. Blend two 3-ounce packages softened cream cheese, ¼ cup milk, and 2 tablespoons mayonnaise; spoon atop gelatin. Swirl the gelatin mixture to marble. Chill till the apple salad is firm. Makes 9 servings.

Cinnamon Popcorn Balls

    3 quarts popped corn
      Butter or margarine
    1 cup sugar
    ⅔ cup red cinnamon candies
    1 tablespoon vinegar
    ¼ teaspoon salt
    1 or 2 drops oil of cinnamon

Keep popped corn hot in very slow oven (200° to 250°). Rub butter on sides of a medium saucepan; in it combine sugar, cinnamon candies, ⅔ cup water, vinegar, and salt. Cook to hard-ball stage (250°), stirring till sugar and candies dissolve. Add oil of cinnamon.

Pour syrup slowly over hot popped corn, mixing well. Butter hands. Press coated popcorn lightly into 2½-inch balls.

RECONSTITUTE—To restore a concentrated liquid to its original proportions. For example, frozen orange juice or frozen grape juice is reconstituted to its natural concentration by the addition of a specified amount of water.

RED PEPPER—1. A spice that is ground from red *Capsicum* peppers. 2. Any sweet or hot, red-colored vegetable pepper that is of the *Capsicum* family.

The seasoning called red pepper is often labeled "cayenne pepper" as well as "red pepper," even though originally they were two distinct spices. When first manufactured, red pepper was made from milder-flavored peppers than cayenne. Now, the terms and the spices are interchangeable.

The vegetables referred to as red peppers are more often considered to be hot varieties—cayenne, chili, Tabasco, and bird peppers—rather than sweet varieties. If allowed to fully ripen, however, some sweet ones turn red and are thus called red peppers. These include the red bell and paprika peppers. Because of this broad terminology, red peppers may be very small or large, and mild or extremely hot.

The hot red peppers are a characteristic food used in the cooking of Central and South America, the Caribbean islands, India, Africa, Indonesia, and Korea. Sweet red peppers are a brilliant color substitute for sweet green peppers and taste much the same. (See also *Cayenne Pepper*, *Pepper* for additional information.)

Jellied Potato Salad

    5 cups diced, peeled, cooked
        potatoes
    1 tablespoon vinegar
    1 cup chopped onion
    1½ cups mayonnaise or salad dressing
    1 tablespoon celery seed
            . . .
    2 3-ounce packages lemon-flavored
        gelatin
    ¼ cup vinegar
    9 green pepper rings
    9 red pepper rings *or* pimiento
        strips
    1 cup diced cucumber

Sprinkle potatoes with the 1 tablespoon vinegar and 2 teaspoons salt. Toss with onion, mayonnaise, and celery seed; chill. Dissolve gelatin in 2½ cups boiling water; stir in the ¼ cup vinegar. To *half* the gelatin mixture add ¼ cup cold water. Pour into a 9x9x2-inch pan. Chill till partially set; arrange peppers atop gelatin. Chill till *almost* firm.

Meanwhile, chill remaining gelatin till partially set; beat till soft peaks form. Fold in potato mixture and cucumber. Spoon over gelatin in pan; chill till firm. Invert to unmold. Cut in squares. Makes 9 servings.

RED PERCH—Another name for the freshwater yellow perch. (See also *Perch*.)

RED SNAPPER—A bright red, lean fish with a juicy, delicate flavor. These fish, weighing as much as 30 pounds and measuring up to 2 feet long, are commonly found in the Gulf of Mexico and around Florida.

Red snappers, usually weighing ½ to 5 pounds, are available in food and fish stores in fresh and frozen forms, including whole or dressed fish, fillets, and portions Any of these forms can be fried, boiled, steamed, or made into soup. With the addition of butter or shortening, they can also be baked or broiled. Baked red snapper is considered a choice entrée as are snapper throats. The flavor of these throats is similar to that of the white meat around the breast bone in a chicken.

Since the red snapper is available all year and is shipped to all parts of the country, this fish can be included in menus during any season and in any place.

Red snapper is a rich source of protein. It also supplies some minerals and the B vitamins thiamine and riboflavin. A 3½-ounce serving of uncooked red snapper yields about 95 calories. (See also *Fish*.)

Snapper with Cashews

```
2  pounds fresh or frozen red snapper
     steaks or other fish steaks
2  tablespoons butter or margarine,
     melted
2  cups soft bread crumbs (3 slices)
¼  cup chopped cashew nuts
½  teaspoon seasoned salt
   Dash pepper
¼  cup butter or margarine, melted
```

Thaw frozen fish. Cut fish into 6 portions. Sprinkle with salt and arrange in a greased 9x9x2-inch baking pan. Drizzle 2 tablespoons butter over fish. Combine crumbs, nuts, seasoned salt, and pepper; add remaining ¼ cup melted butter. Sprinkle crumb mixture over fish. Bake at 350° till fish flakes easily when tested with a fork, 25 to 30 minutes. Serves 6.

REDUCE—To boil down a broth of other liquid to decrease the amount and to concentrate the flavor. This process is used in making sauces to yield a richer flavor.

RED WINE—A wine made from red or black grapes and fermented with the grape skins, which provide the color and other characteristic constituents. Burgundy and Claret are examples of red wines.

As red wine ferments, the grape skins and pulp float on top and form a layer called a "cap" over the wine. In order to distribute the flavor contained in this cap throughout the wine, the wine usually is pumped over the cap or the mixture is punched down or stirred. At the completion of fermentation, the wine is drained off, leaving the pulp and skins behind. Then, the wine is aged, bottled, and labeled before it reaches the consumer.

Although some red wines are used as appetizer and dessert wines, most red wines are used as a main course table wine. Since these table wines, as a class, are generally dry and full-flavored, they most often are served with hearty meats such as beef, pork, veal, and game. Besides their use as a beverage, red wines also add a delightful flavor to a variety of dishes. (See also *Wines and Spirits*.)

Spicy Rump Roast

```
1  3- to 4-pound beef rump roast
2  tablespoons shortening
½  teaspoon dried marjoram leaves,
     crushed
1  8-ounce can tomatoes
½  cup dry red wine
½  cup chopped onion
¼  cup chopped green pepper
1  clove garlic, crushed
1  tablespoon sugar
⅛  teaspoon ground cinnamon
   Dash ground cloves
¼  cup all-purpose flour
```

In Dutch oven slowly brown roast in hot shortening. Season with 1 teaspoon salt and marjoram. Add remaining ingredients except flour. Cover tightly; cook slowly till tender, 2¼ to 2½ hours. Remove the roast to platter.

To make gravy, pour pan juices into large measuring cup; skim off excess fat. Return 1½ cups juices to pan. Blend ½ cup cold water with flour; add to juices. Cook and stir till thickened and bubbly. Makes 8 servings.

Rotisserie Rib Roast Barbecue

½ cup red Burgundy
½ cup vinegar
½ cup salad oil
¼ cup finely chopped onion
2 tablespoons sugar
1 tablespoon Worcestershire sauce
½ teaspoon dry mustard
¼ teaspoon chili powder
⅛ teaspoon dried thyme leaves,
   crushed
1 clove garlic, minced
5 drops bottled hot pepper sauce
1 5- to 6-pound rolled beef
   rib roast

Combine all ingredients *except* roast with 1½ teaspoons salt and ½ teaspoon pepper; marinate roast for 2 hours at room temperature or overnight in refrigerator. Drain, reserving marinade. Insert spit rod through center of roast and adjust holding forks; test balance. Insert meat thermometer. Attach spit and turn on motor (have medium coals at rear of firebox and a drip pan under meat). Lower hood; roast for 2½ to 3 hours for medium-rare doneness, brushing with marinade last ½ hour. Thermometer should register 140° for rare, 160° for medium, 170° for well-done.

Meatballs à la Burgundy

1 beaten egg
½ cup milk
⅓ cup quick-cooking rolled oats
¼ cup finely chopped onion
1 pound ground beef
2 tablespoons shortening
¼ cup all-purpose flour
½ cup red Burgundy
2 beef bouillon cubes
1 teaspoon sugar
1 teaspoon Kitchen Bouquet

Combine first 4 ingredients and ½ teaspoon salt. Add beef; mix well. Shape into 24 balls; brown in hot shortening in skillet. Remove balls; reserve drippings. Stir flour into reserved drippings. Add 2 cups water, wine, and bouillon cubes; cook and stir till bubbly. Stir in remaining ingredients; add meatballs. Cover; simmer 20 minutes. Serves 6.

REFLECTOR OVEN—A portable oven used in campfire cookery for baking breads, pies, and cookies. The most common design for a reflector oven features one shelf set horizontally between two inclined, shiny, metal surfaces. Heat is obtained by setting the open front of the oven so that it faces a flaming campfire. The shiny, metal interior of the oven reflects and intensifies the heat, which provides heat for baking.

To make these ovens more efficient, focus more heat into the oven by building the fire against a ledge or backdrop of green sticks. (See also *Campfire Cookery*.)

REFRIED BEANS—Another name for frijoles refritos. (See also *Frijoles Refritos*.)

REFRIGERATED BISCUITS AND ROLLS—Commercially prepared bread products, usually sold in a tube, that are ready for baking as purchased. These convenience products include plain biscuits, sweet rolls flavored with cinnamon, butterscotch, or orange, and at least one type designed for shaping into crescent rolls. Besides being used separately as dinner rolls or sweet rolls, refrigerated biscuits and rolls are also shortcuts for casserole toppers, coffee cakes, desserts, and other quick bread fix-ups. (See also *Bread*.)

Caramel-Apple Whirls

Start with refrigerated caramel nut rolls—

1 21-ounce can apple pie filling
½ cup fruit juice (orange, pineapple,
   or other)
2 tablespoons butter or margarine
⅓ cup chopped pecans
1 package refrigerated caramel
   nut rolls (8 rolls)

• • •

Dairy sour cream

In saucepan combine apple pie filling, fruit juice, butter or margarine, chopped pecans, and topping mix from the caramel rolls. Bring to boiling. Pour into an 11x7x1½-inch baking pan. Top with caramel rolls. Bake at 375° till done, about 20 to 25 minutes. Serve warm topped with dairy sour cream. Makes 8 servings.

Pizza Pronto

>   2 8-ounce packages refrigerated
>   biscuits
>   1 8-ounce can tomato sauce
>   1 teaspoon instant minced onion
>   ¼ teaspoon ground oregano
>   ¼ teaspoon garlic salt
>   1 4-ounce package shredded sharp
>   Cheddar cheese (1 cup)
>   2 slices mozzarella cheese, torn
>   in pieces
>   1 6-ounce can mushroom crowns,
>   drained
>   ½ cup pitted ripe olives, halved
>   lengthwise (optional)

With palms of hands, flatten refrigerated biscuits into 4½x2-inch ovals. On greased baking sheet, stagger 10 biscuits in 2 rows so that narrow ends fit between space left between biscuits in other row. Press adjoining ends together securely. Repeat with remaining biscuits.

Combine tomato sauce, instant minced onion, ground oregano, and garlic salt; spread mixture evenly over biscuits to within ½ inch of edges. Sprinkle with shredded sharp Cheddar cheese; top with mozzarella cheese pieces. Arrange mushroom crowns atop the cheese.

Bake at 450° till edges of crusts are brown, about 8 to 10 minutes. If desired, garnish with ripe olive halves. Makes 2 pizzas.

Quick Apple Dumplings

>   1 21-ounce can apple pie filling
>   2½ cups water
>   ½ cup raisins
>   ⅓ cup red cinnamon candies
>   ⅓ cup sugar
>   ¼ cup chopped nuts
>   2 tablespoons butter or margarine
>   1 tablespoon lemon juice
>   1 package refrigerated cinnamon
>   rolls with icing (8 rolls)

In electric skillet combine all ingredients *except* rolls. Cook and stir till butter melts and mixture is bubbly. Arrange rolls atop filling. Cover; with lid vent open cook at 250° till rolls are done, 20 to 25 minutes. Spread icing from package over rolls. Serve warm with cream, if desired. Makes 8 servings.

Quicky Crullers

Unroll one tube refrigerated crescent rolls (8 rolls). Pinch together diagonal perforations of each 2 crescents, making 4 rectangles. Cut in thirds lengthwise. Tie each strip in knot. Fry in deep hot fat (375°) till browned. Drain. While warm, brush with confectioners' sugar frosting (see *Confectioners' Sugar*).

Parmesan Biscuits

>   ¼ cup butter or margarine, melted
>   2 tablespoons snipped parsley
>   1 clove garlic, minced
>
>   • • •
>
>   2 packages refrigerated biscuits
>   (20 biscuits)
>   ¼ cup grated Parmesan cheese

Mix melted butter or margarine, snipped parsley, and minced garlic. Dip biscuits in butter mixture. Overlap 15 biscuits around edge and rest of biscuits in center of well-greased 9x1½-inch round pan. Top with remaining butter mixture and Parmesan cheese. Bake at 425° for 15 minutes. Remove from pan at once.

REFRIGERATOR CAKE—A chilled dessert that is made with pieces of cake or cookies and a puddinglike mixture. As the dessert chills, the cake or cookies absorb the pudding mixture until the two parts are blended into a moist, flavorful whole.

Cherry-Angel Dessert

A delicious make-ahead dessert—

>   8 cups ½-inch cubes angel cake
>   1 21-ounce can cherry pie filling
>   1 3¾- or 3⅝-ounce package
>   *instant* vanilla pudding mix
>   1½ cups milk
>   1 cup dairy sour cream

Place *half* the angel cake cubes in 9x9x2-inch pan. Spoon pie filling over cake. Top with remaining cake. Combine pudding mix, milk, and sour cream; beat smooth. Spoon over cake. Chill 5 hours. Makes 9 servings.

Chocolate-Angel Delight

Mold this rich, delicious refrigerator cake in a decorative mold for an extra-special dessert—

  1 envelope unflavored gelatin
        (1 tablespoon)
  ½ cup cold water
  1 package fluffy chocolate
        frosting mix
  1 cup whipping cream
  4 cups angel cake cubes
  ¼ cup chopped peanuts
        Chopped peanuts

Soften unflavored gelatin in cold water; dissolve over hot water. Remove from heat and set aside. Prepare fluffy chocolate frosting mix according to package directions; blend in dissolved gelatin. Chill, stirring constantly, till mixture mounds when spooned.

Whip cream; fold into chocolate mixture with angel cake cubes. Sprinkle ¼ cup chopped peanuts in bottom of oiled 5½- to 6-cup mold. Spoon in chilled chocolate mixture. Chill till firm, at least 5 hours or overnight. Carefully unmold on serving plate; top with additional chopped peanuts. Makes 8 servings.

REFRIGERATOR COOKIES—Crisp cookies made from dough that is shaped in rolls and chilled thoroughly before it is thinly sliced and baked. (See also *Cookies.*)

Flossie the Fish

The kids will love these—

Cut eighteen ¼-inch slices from roll of refrigerated slice-and-bake sugar cookie dough. For body of fish, make a slit in 12 of the cookie slices, *cutting just from edge to center.* Place cookies, 2 inches apart, on *ungreased* cookie sheet, spreading slits apart slightly to make mouths. Cut remaining cookie slices in sixths. Arrange these wedges around body of fish to make tails and fins; don't crowd various pieces together—barely touching is close enough. Press on silver decorettes for eyes. Bake as directed on package. Cool 1 minute; remove to rack. Repeat the process with the remaining dough. Makes about 3 dozen cookies.

Chocolate Pinwheels

One cookie with two colors and flavors—

  ½ cup butter or margarine
  ¾ cup sugar
  2 teaspoons vanilla
  1 egg
        • • •
  1¾ cups sifted all-purpose flour
  ½ teaspoon baking powder
  ½ teaspoon salt
  1 1-ounce square unsweetened
        chocolate, melted
        Milk

In mixing bowl cream butter or margarine, sugar, and vanilla till light and fluffy; beat in egg. Sift together dry ingredients; mix into creamed mixture. Divide dough in half; mix melted chocolate into one part.

On waxed paper, roll each half of dough into a 12x10-inch rectangle. (Piece dough together, if necessary, to make rectangle.) Brush one layer with milk; place other layer on top. Peel off waxed paper. Roll as for jelly roll. Wrap in waxed paper. Chill thoroughly. Slice thin; bake on *ungreased* cookie sheet at 375° for 8 to 10 minutes. Makes 4 to 6 dozen.

Slice Orange Refrigerator Cookies thinly so they will be crisp. Fresh orange juice and peel give the cookies a refreshing flavor.

Orange Refrigerator Cookies

Nuts add texture—

1 cup butter or margarine
½ cup granulated sugar
½ cup brown sugar
1 egg
1 tablespoon grated orange peel
¼ cup orange juice
1 teaspoon vanilla

. . .

3 cups sifted all-purpose flour
½ teaspoon salt
¼ teaspoon baking soda
½ cup chopped walnuts

In mixing bowl thoroughly cream butter, granulated sugar, and brown sugar; add egg, grated orange peel, orange juice, and vanilla. Beat well. Sift together all-purpose flour, salt, and baking soda; add to creamed mixture, mixing well. Stir in chopped nuts. Shape into rolls 2 inches in diameter. Wrap in waxed paper and chill thoroughly. Slice thinly; about ⅛ inch thick. Bake on *ungreased* cookie sheet at 375° for 12 to 15 minutes. Makes 8 dozen.

Orange-Ginger Cookies

Serve these with hot tea—

1 cup butter or margarine
1½ cups sugar
1 egg
2 tablespoons light corn syrup
3 cups sifted all-purpose flour
2 teaspoons baking soda
2 teaspoons ground cinnamon
2 teaspoons ground ginger
½ teaspoon ground cloves
1 tablespoon shredded orange peel

In mixing bowl thoroughly cream together butter and sugar. Add egg and syrup; beat well. Sift together flour, baking soda, cinnamon, ginger, and cloves; mix into creamed mixture along with orange peel. Shape into two 9-inch rolls about 2 inches in diameter. Wrap in waxed paper; chill several hours or overnight. Slice about ⅛ inch thick. Place 2 inches apart on *ungreased* cookie sheet. Bake at 400° till done, about 5 to 6 minutes. Makes about 8 dozen.

REFRIGERATOR DESSERT—Any of several types of desserts that require chilling in the refrigerator. Whipped cream and gelatin are ingredients frequently used in this kind of dessert. Refrigerator desserts, particularly appealing to the hurried hostess, can be prepared ahead and then refrigerated until serving time. (See also *Dessert*.)

Chilled Banana Cheesecake

1 cup graham cracker crumbs
¼ cup sugar
¼ teaspoon ground cinnamon
¼ cup butter or margarine, melted
¾ cup sugar
2 envelopes unflavored gelatin
      (2 tablespoons)
¼ teaspoon salt
2 beaten egg yolks
1 6-ounce can evaporated milk
      (⅔ cup)
1 teaspoon grated lemon peel
2 13-ounce cartons cream-style
      cottage cheese, sieved
1½ teaspoons vanilla
1 cup mashed banana
1 tablespoon lemon juice
2 egg whites
¼ cup sugar
1 cup whipping cream

For crust, combine graham cracker crumbs, ¼ cup sugar, and cinnamon. Blend in melted butter. Lightly butter sides of an 8-inch springform pan; reserve ¼ of the crumb mixture and firmly press the remaining crumb mixture onto bottom and sides of the springform pan.

For filling, combine ¾ cup sugar, gelatin, and salt in heavy saucepan. Stir in egg yolks and milk. Cook and stir till gelatin dissolves and mixture thickens slightly, 5 to 10 minutes. Remove from heat. Add lemon peel; cool.

Stir in cottage cheese and vanilla. Chill, stirring occasionally, till partially set. Combine mashed banana and lemon juice; fold into gelatin mixture. Beat egg whites to soft peaks. Slowly add the ¼ cup sugar, beating to stiff peaks; fold into gelatin mixture. Whip cream; fold cream into gelatin mixture.

Pour filling into crumb-lined pan. Sprinkle with reserved crumbs. Chill till firm, 6 to 8 hours or overnight. Makes 12 servings.

REGIONAL COOKERY

"As American as apple pie" is a phrase often used to describe something that is considered typical of all the United States. Although apple pie is served throughout this country, many other dishes are considered specialties of specific areas. In fact, a close examination reveals that just about every village and town has a food specialty. However, there are common characteristics and foods that tend to divide the United States into four general culinary regions—Northeast, South, Midwest, and Southwest-West.

Describe your favorite dishes, and you more than likely give a clue to which part of the nation you are from. For example, a fondness for slow-cooked baked beans indicates that you are from New England, while a craving for scrapple comes from a Pennsylvania Dutch background. If sweet potato pie is high on your list of favorites, no doubt you're from the South. A longing for a grilled beef steak denotes that you were brought up in the Midwest, while a love of barbecue feasts places you with other Texans. Natives of the states that border Mexico undoubtedly will express a preference for foods that show a Mexican influence. And if you were raised on the West Coast, Dungeness crab and abalone are probably favorites of yours.

These examples, however, are only a few of the many foods and dishes that typify the four regions of this country. A more extensive culinary journey will uncover many other regional characteristics.

Steak southwestern style

← Tender Ranch House Round Steak served with cornbread and Texas-Style Beans (see *Pinto Bean* for recipe) make a hearty meal.

Northeastern

This region extends from the northern east coast, with its bountiful fish and seafood, inland to Pennsylvania where the food of the Pennsylvania Dutch is at home. Although fine food is plentiful in this region, the foods of three distinctive cuisines—New England, Shaker, and Pennsylvania Dutch—best illustrate northeastern cookery.

New England: The mention of New England's food invariably brings to mind baked beans. Rich with a flavor acquired through hours of baking, Boston baked beans are indeed a classic. However, New England cooks are also noted for numerous other good foods.

The close proximity of the Atlantic Ocean has resulted in a large number of New England fish and seafood dishes. Saltwater fish are deliciously cooked in many ways, and lobsters are boiled, broiled, or baked and made into bisque, chowder, stew, and pie. There are all types of fish and seafood chowders, but the most famous of these is clam chowder. This dish is made with milk everywhere in New England except in Rhode Island where Manhattan-style chowder with tomato is preferred.

New England is also noted for its cranberry bogs. These bogs produce thousands of pounds of berries yearly. Although this crop is shipped throughout the United States, New Englanders keep part of the berries for use in pies, cakes, breads, ice creams, sherbets, and sauces.

The New Englanders' traditional thriftiness is exemplified by their boiled dinner of corned beef and root vegetables, which is served fresh. Later, the leftovers become red flannel hash. Thrifty and good, too, are a salt fish dinner of cod, and crisp, fried salt pork in milk gravy.

Other specialties of this area include molasses doughnuts spiced with cinnamon and ginger, anadama bread flavored with molasses and cornmeal, and squash muffins and biscuits. And don't forget gingerbread, Hartford election cake, and old-fashioned Indian pudding with ice cream on top.

Shaker: During the mid-1700s, a band of religious people called Shakers established several colonies in the New England area. Although these colonies are no longer active, Shaker recipes have survived as part of the cuisine typical of this region.

The relatively simple foods of these people were prepared almost entirely from their farm crops and foods found in the woodlands. During the growing season, fruits and vegetables were used fresh and large quantities of these were also canned for use during the long winter. Milk, cream, butter, and lard were used extensively as ingredients as were a wide variety of herbs grown in large herb gardens.

The Shakers were excellent bakers, too. White and whole wheat bread, salt-rising bread, potato bread, and muffins were a common part of the Shaker diet. Cakes and pies, sometimes sweetened with maple sugar, honey, or molasses, where also frequently prepared. Rosewater and herbs were favorite flavorings for cakes and cookies.

Pennsylvania Dutch: Down the coast and inland a bit from New England, Pennsylvania Dutch cooks set lavish tables with hearty German-style foods. For breakfast there is scrapple, fried liver pudding, or any of a number of sausages as a change from eggs. Buckwheat grows well in Pennsylvania, so a jug of starter for buckwheat batter is kept from October to May for winter pancakes. Some of the soups these cooks make from noodles and an abundance of vegetables, are hearty enough to be the supper main dish. Creamed or buttered vegetables with a touch of herb, coleslaw, or wilted lettuce, and, maybe a bowl of cottage cheese also help tame the appetite. A selection of sweets such as jams, jellies, or preserves, and sours ranging from mustard pickles to pickled cherries is always there to "make things taste good." In this area, all the food for a meal, soup through dessert (often shoofly pie), is placed on the table at once so that each person can see what's there and tailor his servings to the size of his appetite.

New England Dinner

    1 small clove garlic
    1 bay leaf
 2½ pounds corned beef
    6 small potatoes, peeled and
       halved
    1 small rutabaga *or* turnip,
       cut in chunks
    6 medium carrots, peeled and
       halved
    1 small head cabbage, quartered
    4 peppercorns

Place 1 cup water, garlic, and bay leaf in a 6-quart pressure pan with rack. Place meat on rack. Close cover securely. Cook 45 minutes at 15 pounds pressure. Let pressure drop of its own accord. Open pan and add potatoes, rutabaga, carrots, cabbage, and peppercorns. Close cover securely and return pan to heat. Cook 6 to 7 minutes at 15 pounds pressure. Reduce pressure quickly by placing under cold running water. Makes 6 servings.

Rosewater and Caraway Cookies

    1 cup butter or margarine
    1 cup sugar
    2 beaten eggs
 2¾ cups sifted all-purpose flour
    1 teaspoon baking soda
  ½ teaspoon cream of tartar
  ½ cup mixed, chopped, candied
       fruits and peels
  ½ cup light raisins
    2 tablespoons caraway seed
    2 tablespoons rosewater

Cream first 3 ingredients till light and fluffy. Sift together flour, soda, cream of tartar, and dash salt; add to creamed mixture. Stir in remaining ingredients. Drop from teaspoon onto *ungreased* cookie sheet. Flatten with glass dipped in flour; center each with a light raisin. Bake at 375° till lightly browned, 8 to 10 minutes. Cool on rack. Makes about 4½ dozen.

Mennonite Chicken with Sour Cream

　¼ cup butter or margarine
　¼ cup all-purpose flour
　1 teaspoon salt
　1 2-pound ready-to-cook broiler-
　　　fryer chicken, split in half
　　Paprika
　　　　. . .
　3 tablespoons water
　1 tablespoon all-purpose flour
　¼ teaspoon salt
　　Dash pepper
　　Dash paprika
　½ cup dairy sour cream

Place butter in shallow baking pan or oven-going skillet; heat to melt butter. Combine ¼ cup flour, salt, and dash pepper; roll chicken in mixture till coated. Dip coated chicken in melted butter and arrange, skin side up, in the baking pan. Sprinkle with paprika. Bake at 325° till the chicken is tender and nicely browned, about 1¼ hours. Remove the chicken from the baking pan; keep the chicken warm.

Add water to pan drippings; mix well. Blend in remaining ingredients. Bring just to boiling, stirring constantly. Remove from heat and serve over chicken. Makes 2 servings.

Southern

The area known as the South extends down the Atlantic coast from Maryland to Florida and then westward through Louisiana. Seafood is plentiful and southern cooks excel in preparing it. Other specialties include fried chicken and baked goods.

One of the outstanding characteristics of the cookery of this area is the great influence exerted by immigrants. For example, English influence is evident in Maryland and Virginia, while Louisiana shows both French and Spanish influences.

All through the South there is evidence of the influence of Afro-American cooks who created specialties from the foods of the region. These cooks are credited with developing many of the southern dishes using sweet potatoes and peanuts as well as dishes such as gumbo and chitterlings.

Since the majority of southern states border the ocean, fish and seafood are important in this cuisine. Crab is fixed in numerous ways in Maryland and the Carolinas, from plain, boiled hard-shells to delicate crab timbales. Oysters are scalloped in Virginia, baked with spinach in New Orleans, and fried, broiled, or made into soups everywhere. There are okra-flavored gumbos of shrimp, crab, or lobster, and shrimp is also found in pilaf, with corn in a pie, or crumb-coated and fried.

Southern fried chicken is popularly prepared throughout the South. Although some cooks flour the chicken for frying, others prefer crumbing. Still others like to coat it with a batter dip. But, no matter which technique is used, the chicken typically turns out moist and delicious. Another meat favorite in this area is smoked ham, which is served with "red-eye" gravy.

Southern cooks are great bakers, too. Tiny baking powder biscuits, all flaky crust with almost no "innards," melt like snowflakes when eaten. By contrast, southern cornbread is plain, unsweetened, and unleavened, and beaten biscuits are reminiscent of thick, though tender, crackers. Other hot bread favorites include spoon bread, buttermilk batter bread, and crackling bread. Regional sweet baked specialties include sweet potato pie, pecan pie, and the elegant Lady Baltimore cake.

The favorite vegetables of this region include rice and hominy grits. The ever-popular sweet potato is served baked, boiled, fried, mashed, and candied. Turnip, mustard, and collard greens as well as spinach and green beans are usually cooked with a piece of salt pork or ham.

In the Gulf states, particularly southeastern Louisiana, the descendants of French and Spanish settlers, called Creoles, have developed a distinctive cuisine. The frequent use of fish, shellfish, game, rice, and vegetables such as okra and tomatoes typifies the foods of the Creoles. One of the most important parts of this cuisine is the *roux*. This cooked flour-shortening mixture is the basis for many thickened soups, sauces, and seafood dishes.

Most of the flavorful Creole dishes are highly seasoned with a combination of herbs and spices. The seasoning that is most distinctively Creole is filé (powdered sassafras leaves), which is popularly used in seafood dishes and gumbos.

Bacon Spoon Bread

¾ cup cornmeal
1½ cups cold water
8 ounces sharp natural Cheddar
  cheese, shredded (2 cups)
¼ cup butter, softened
2 cloves garlic, crushed
½ teaspoon salt
1 cup milk
4 well-beaten egg yolks
8 ounces sliced bacon, crisp-
  cooked and drained
4 stiffly beaten egg whites

Combine cornmeal and water; cook, stirring constantly, till the mixture is consistency of mush. Remove from heat. Add cheese, butter, garlic, and salt; stir to melt cheese. Gradually add milk. Stir in egg yolks.

Crumble bacon, reserving some for garnish; add to cornmeal mixture. Fold in egg whites. Pour into greased 2-quart soufflé dish. Bake at 325° till done, about 65 minutes. Spoon into warm dishes; top with butter. Serves 6.

Oysters Bienville

Open 18 oysters in shells. With knife, remove oysters. Wash shells. Place each oyster in deep half of the shell. Arrange shells on bed of rock salt in a shallow pan; set aside.

Cook ½ cup chopped green onion and 1 clove garlic, minced, in 2 tablespoons butter or margarine till tender but not brown. Blend in 2 tablespoons all-purpose flour and ¼ teaspoon salt. Add ⅔ cup chicken broth all at once. Cook and stir till mixture thickens and bubbles.

Beat 1 egg yolk and ⅓ cup dry white wine together. Add a little of hot mixture to egg and wine; return to hot mixture. Stir in one 3-ounce can sliced mushrooms, drained; 2 tablespoons snipped parsley; and dash bottled hot pepper sauce. Cook and stir till almost boiling.

In small saucepan melt ½ tablespoon butter; add ½ cup soft bread crumbs (1 slice) and toss to coat. Stir in 2 tablespoons grated Parmesan cheese. Heat oysters at 400° for 5 minutes. Top each oyster with 1 tablespoon of the sauce mixture. Sprinkle 1 teaspoon bread-Parmesan mixture atop each oyster. Bake till heated through and crumbs are lightly browned, about 10 to 12 minutes longer. Makes 6 servings.

Pecan Pralines

3 cups sugar
1 teaspoon baking soda
1 cup buttermilk
¾ cup light corn syrup
2 tablespoons butter or margarine
2 cups pecan halves

In large saucepan or Dutch oven combine sugar, baking soda, and ⅛ teaspoon salt. Stir in buttermilk and corn syrup. Bring to boiling over medium heat, stirring constantly. Cook and stir to soft-ball stage (234°). Remove from heat; add butter. Stir in pecans; beat till mixture is thick enough to drop from spoon, 5 to 6 minutes. Quickly drop from tablespoon onto waxed paper. If candy becomes too stiff, add 1 teaspoon hot water. Makes about 45.

Midwestern

The large area called the Midwest extends from Ohio to California and from Canada to Oklahoma. Like all of the other regions, this area is very diverse. However, the cuisine of the Midwest is banded together by the use of the crops and livestock that thrive on the farms and ranches of this area. Another quality of the Midwest that is often overlooked is the retention of immigrant cuisines in settlements scattered throughout this region. For example, the Germans and Scandinavians in the northern states, the Dutch in Michigan, and the polyglot of nationalities in Chicago have not only retained many of their native foods but have also introduced many dishes into the general cuisine of this region.

The Midwest is corn country, with roasting ears aplenty, custardy corn pudding, corn fried with onions and green peppers, and even corn chowder. It is wheat country, too, with tables plenteously supplied with breads and coffee cakes reminiscent of the baking of many lands. There are dumplings both hearty and sweet, numerous dishes that make use of the dairy products of the Midwest, pasta made of locally grown hard wheat, and numerous delicious pies, cakes, cookies, and other baked goods.

Midwestern cooks who know how to cook the beef of Kansas, Nebraska, and Iowa do equally well with a New York-style sirloin or an economical chicken-fried steak. They roast the pork of Iowa to succulent perfection, and they are only slightly fazed by the prospect of cooking a bear or buffalo pot roast, elkburgers, or antelope chops. The lakes and rivers of the area abound with fish, which are baked, broiled, or panbroiled. This in an area of hearty food, which is prepared simply to bring out the food's basic good quality.

Fresh Peach Ice Cream

> 1¼ cups sugar
> 1½ teaspoons unflavored gelatin
> 4 cups light cream
> 1 slightly beaten egg
> 1 teaspoon vanilla
> ¼ teaspoon almond extract
> 6 peaches, peeled, seeded, and mashed (3 cups)

In saucepan combine ½ cup sugar and gelatin. Stir in *half* the cream. Stir over low heat till gelatin dissolves. Slowly blend small amount of hot mixture into beaten egg; return to hot mixture. Cook and stir till slightly thickened, about 1 minute. Chill. Add remaining cream, vanilla, almond extract, and dash salt. Combine mashed peaches and the remaining sugar; add to chilled gelatin-cream mixture.

Pour into ice cream freezer can. (Fill can only ⅔ full to allow for expansion during freezing.) Fit can into freezer. Adjust dasher and cover. Pack crushed ice and rock salt around can, using proportions of 6 parts ice to 1 part salt. (Pack ice and salt up to—but not over—lid of can.) *Turn handle slowly till ice melts and forms brine; add more ice and salt throughout freezing to maintain ice level. Turn handle at constant speed till crank becomes difficult to turn. Remove ice to a level below the lid of freezer can; thoroughly wipe cover and top of freezer can. Remove lid; pull out and scrape dasher. Makes about 2 quarts.

To ripen ice cream: Plug opening in lid. Pack more ice and salt (using proportion of 4 parts ice to 1 part rock salt) around freezer can to fill freezer. Cover with heavy cloth or newspapers. Let ripen for at least 4 hours to improve and mellow the flavor.

*If using electric ice cream freezer, follow manufacturer's directions.

Six-Layer Dinner

Layer the following in a 3-quart casserole, seasoning each layer with salt and pepper: 3 cups sliced, peeled, raw potatoes; one 17-ounce can whole kernel corn, drained; 1 medium onion, sliced; 1 pound ground beef; and 1 cup sliced raw carrots. Pour one 16-ounce can tomatoes, cut up, over casserole. Cover and bake at 350° about 1¾ hours. Serves 6.

Quick Corn Chowder

In large saucepan cook 5 slices bacon till crisp. Remove bacon; crumble and set aside. Reserve 3 tablespoons drippings in saucepan; discard remainder. Add 1 medium onion, sliced and separated into rings; cook till lightly browned. Add 2 medium potatoes, peeled and diced, and ½ cup water; cook over medium heat till potato is tender, 10 to 15 minutes.

Add one 17-ounce can cream-style corn, 2 cups milk, 1 teaspoon salt, and dash pepper; cook till heated through. Pour into warmed bowls; top each serving with crumbled bacon and a pat of butter or margarine. Serve with crackers, if desired. Makes 4 or 5 servings.

Southwestern and Western

This region of the United States includes eight states—Texas, New Mexico, Arizona, California, Oregon, Washington, Alaska, and Hawaii. Since this region includes so many different types of cookery, it is further divided into the southwestern states, the Pacific coast states, Alaska, and Hawaii.

Southwest: The cookery of the southwestern states is influenced by Mexican and Indian foods. Tortillas, tamales, and tacos are as much at home here as south of the border. Corn, the basic grain, is used in the all-purpose corn flour dough. Hot chili peppers, hung to dry in the sun, are used to season corn, bean, and meat dishes. Chili powder mixtures, too, are used for pungent seasoning. From the Indians come sage-flavored honey for sweetening, pine nuts to add flavor and texture, and cookery with cornmeal as an Apache bread. Other Indian contributions are acorn soup, fried bread dough, and jerky stew.

Texas is barbecue country, with anything from a whole steer to a hamburger skillfully grilled and sauced. However, Texas cookery also includes typical southern dishes and many Mexican dishes. Frijoles and candied yams are as much at home here as are ranch house beans. And, backing up the Texan's claim that everything is richer in Texas, pecan pie is made there with more butter and eggs than elsewhere.

Pacific coast: This area has several foods that deserve special mention. Seafood is king—crabs, clams, oysters, and fish. Crab Louis originated in Seattle, and both Dungeness and king crabs are cooked and served in dozens of other ways. Special taste treats of this area include barbecued salmon up north, cioppino (fish stew) in San Francisco, and grilled abalone from southern California. Throughout the area, oriental foods are popular. And sourdough bread has had a revival in California.

Alaska and Hawaii: Both of these states are separated from the other states by such great distances that they are not really tied to the cuisine typical of the western region. Alaskans enjoy dishes that are not available in other parts of the country, such as mooseburgers, reindeer steaks, and ptarmigan stew. Fish, seafood, and native berries and vegetables are also commonly used by Alaskan cooks. Unlike the cold of Alaska, the climate of Hawaii is tropical. As a result, tropical fruits are used extensively by the Islanders. Hawaiian cookery is also noted for its adoption of dishes brought in by Oriental, Portuguese, and other immigrants to the Islands.

Grilled Abalone

Use 1 pound fresh or frozen abalone steaks (thaw if frozen). Combine 1/3 cup all-purpose flour, 1 teaspoon salt, and 1/4 teaspoon pepper. Combine 1 beaten egg and 1 tablespoon milk. Dip abalone steaks in flour mixture and then in egg mixture. Coat steaks with 1 1/2 cups fine saltine cracker crumbs. Melt 1/4 cup butter or margarine in skillet; cook steaks 1 minute on each side. *Do not overcook.* Drain on paper toweling. Serve piping hot. Makes 4 servings.

Western Salad

Seed, peel, and slice 2 avocados. Prepare 2 cups cantaloupe balls. Cook 6 slices bacon till crisp; drain and crumble. In large salad bowl toss 4 cups shredded lettuce with *half* the avocado, melon, and bacon. Arrange remaining avocado and melon atop; add remaining bacon. Pass sweet French salad dressing. Serves 8.

Ranch House Round Steak

Cut 3 pounds 1/2-inch thick round steak into serving-sized pieces; trim off excess fat and slash edges of meat. Combine 1/4 cup all-purpose flour, 2 teaspoons dry mustard, 1 1/2 teaspoons salt, and 1/8 teaspoon pepper; coat meat with mixture. (Set aside any remaining mixture.)

In heavy skillet brown meat on both sides in 1/4 cup hot salad oil. Add reserved flour mixture to skillet. Combine 1/2 cup water and 1 tablespoon Worcestershire sauce; stir into mixture in skillet. Cover tightly; cook over low heat till meat is tender, 1 to 1 1/4 hours. Remove meat to platter. Skim fat from pan juices; drizzle juices over meat. Serves 8.

Hilo Franks

As shown on the cover—

Combine 1 cup apricot preserves, half of 8-ounce can tomato sauce (1/2 cup), 1/3 cup vinegar, 1/4 cup sherry, 2 tablespoons soy sauce, 2 tablespoons honey, 1 tablespoon salad oil, 1 teaspoon salt, and 1/4 teaspoon ground ginger.

Score 2 pounds frankfurters on the bias and grill slowly over *medium* coals, turning and basting often with the sauce, till hot through and glazed. Last few minutes place one 20-ounce can pineapple slices, drained, on grill; brush with sauce, grill, and turn. Brush again with sauce. Heat remaining sauce to pass with grilled frankfurters. Makes 8 to 10 servings.

Franks with a Hawaiian touch

Glazed with a sweet-sour apricot sauce,→ these Hilo Franks and canned pineapple slices sizzle over the coals on a hibachi.

Today, it is often difficult to define what typifies a region because of the speed of transportation of fresh foods and the population mobility. As people move, they take their food favorites with them.

REHYDRATE—To replace fluid lost during dehydration. Instant nonfat dry milk must be rehydrated before it is drunk.

REINDEER—A deer with branched antlers that lives in the cold, northern parts of the world. The inhabitants of these areas raise reindeer for its pelt amd meat. The delicate, sweet reindeer meat can be prepared similarly to beef or venison, and it is delicious marinated, then braised.

RELISH—A food served as an accompaniment to add color and flavor to a meal. Popular relishes include crisp, raw vegetables—carrot sticks, celery strips, cauliflowerets, pickles, olives—and succulent mixtures of chopped fruits or vegetables such as cranberry relish and corn relish. A piquantly dressed salad, pickled or spiced fruits and vegetables, and applesauce also fall into the relish category. Even catsup and mustard are sometimes considered relishes.

Pickled Apricots

    1 cup dried apricots
    1 cup brown sugar
    ¼ cup vinegar
    2 inches stick cinnamon
    6 whole cloves
    24 to 30 walnut halves

Rinse apricots. In saucepan cover apricots with 1 inch water. Cover and simmer gently for 15 minutes. Drain, reserving ¾ cup apricot liquid. In saucepan combine reserved apricot liquid, brown sugar, vinegar, stick cinnamon, and whole cloves. Stir in apricots; return to boiling and simmer, covered, till the apricots are tender, about 10 minutes more.

Cool apricots in syrup. Refrigerate till ready to serve. At serving time, remove the apricots from the syrup. Fill each apricot half with a walnut half. Makes 2 to 2½ dozen.

Bean Relish

    1 16-ounce can whole green beans
    ⅓ cup vinegar
    2 tablespoons sugar
    1 teaspoon salt
    1 teaspoon dillseed
    1 teaspoon mixed pickling spices
        • • •
    1 medium onion, sliced and
        separated in rings
    1 tablespoon salad oil

Drain beans, reserving liquid. In saucepan combine reserved liquid with vinegar, sugar, salt, dillseed, and mixed pickling spices; simmer 5 minutes. Add beans; heat the mixture through. Cool mixture. Then, drain off excess liquid. Toss beans with onion rings and salad oil. Chill before serving. Makes about 2 cups.

Apple-Pickle Relish

Combine 2 unpeeled tart apples, chopped; ¼ cup chopped onion; and ¼ cup chopped dill pickle. Combine ¼ cup sugar and 2 tablespoons vinegar. Toss with apple mixture; chill the mixture thoroughly. Makes about 3 cups relish.

Confetti Relish

    1 16-ounce can French-style green
        beans, drained
    1 12-ounce can whole kernel corn,
        drained
    1 8½-ounce can peas, drained
    1 6-ounce can sliced mushrooms,
        drained
    ¼ cup chopped onion
    ¼ cup diced canned pimiento
    ⅓ cup white wine vinegar
    ¼ cup sugar
    1 teaspoon salt
    ½ cup salad oil

Combine the first 6 ingredients in a large bowl. In screw-top jar combine vinegar, sugar, and salt; cover and shake till the sugar is dissolved. Add oil and shake the mixture well. Pour oil mixture over vegetable mixture. Chill several hours, stirring occasionally. Drain well before serving. Makes about 5 cups.

Fresh Corn Relish

A summertime favorite—

    4 cups fresh, cut corn (6 to 8
       medium ears)
    2 cups chopped cabbage
    2 tablespoons chopped onion
    ¾ cup vinegar
    ½ cup water
    ½ cup sugar
    ½ envelope French salad dressing
       mix (1 tablespoon)
    ½ cup chopped green pepper
    2 tablespoons chopped canned
       pimiento

In saucepan combine corn, cabbage, onion, vinegar, water, sugar, and salad dressing mix. Simmer about 20 minutes, stirring occasionally. Cool; add chopped green pepper and pimiento. Chill thoroughly. Makes 5 cups relish.

Cranberry-Orange Relish is perfect for holiday gift giving. Tuck a jar inside a grater, and trim with ribbons and stars.

Cranberry-Orange Relish

    1 pound fresh cranberries
    2 cups sugar
    ½ cup water
    1 teaspoon grated orange peel
    ½ cup orange juice
    ½ cup slivered almonds

In saucepan combine cranberries, sugar, water, orange peel, and orange juice. Cook, uncovered, till cranberry skins pop, about 10 minutes, stirring once or twice. Remove mixture from heat. Stir in the almonds. Cool. Store relish in covered container in the refrigerator till ready to serve. Makes about 4 cups relish.

Carrot-Olive Slaw

    ¼ cup salad oil
    2 tablespoons vinegar
    2 tablespoons sugar
    ½ teaspoon salt
       Dash pepper
    3 cups shredded carrots
    ¼ cup sliced pitted ripe olives

Combine salad oil, vinegar, sugar, salt, and pepper. Toss lightly with shredded carrots and sliced olives. Chill. Makes about 2½ cups.

Salsa

Serve this delicious Mexican-style sauce as a relish with meats or omelets—

    4 medium firm, ripe tomatoes,
       peeled and finely chopped
    ½ cup finely chopped onion
    ½ cup finely chopped celery
    ¼ cup finely chopped green pepper
    ¼ cup olive oil or salad oil
    2 tablespoons red wine vinegar
    1 tablespoon mustard seed
    1 teaspoon coriander seed, crushed
    2 to 3 tablespoons drained, canned,
       finely chopped green chilies
    1 teaspoon salt
       Dash pepper

Mix all ingredients together in a bowl. Chill several hours or overnight. Makes 3 cups.

RELLENO *(rāl yā′ nō)*—A Spanish word meaning to stuff or fill. The popular Mexican dish Chilies Rellenos con Queso consists of stuffed chili peppers with cheese.

RÉMOULADE SAUCE *(rā′ muh lȧd′)*—A sharp-flavored sauce based on mayonnaise, anchovies or anchovy paste, capers, gherkins, and chopped herbs. The sauce is often used as an accompaniment.

Artichoke and Crab Rémoulade

      4 **artichokes**
        Lemon juice
        Vinegar
   ¾ **teaspoon dried tarragon leaves, crushed**
   ½ **teaspoon dried chervil leaves, crushed**
      1 **cup mayonnaise**
      1 **tablespoon drained, mashed capers**
      2 **teaspoons prepared mustard**
   ½ **teaspoon anchovy paste**
        Medium-thick tomato slices
        Lettuce cups
      1 **cup drained flaked crab meat**

With a sharp knife cut off stems of artichokes; dip bases in lemon juice to prevent darkening. Remove fuzzy chokes and all leaves. Trim artichoke bottoms to make them sit flat; cut around the outside edges with a circular motion (as if peeling an apple) till light-colored meat is visible. Rub with lemon juice and vinegar.

Cook artichoke bottoms, covered, in a small amount of boiling, salted water till just tender. Chill thoroughly. Meanwhile, combine 1 tablespoon warm water, tarragon, and chervil. Let stand 10 minutes. Blend herbs, mayonnaise, capers, mustard, and anchovy paste. Chill.

To assemble the salads place tomato slices in lettuce cups. Top each salad with a cooked, chilled artichoke bottom, then with about ¼ cup crab meat. Top with sauce; garnish with capers, if desired. Makes 4 servings.

RENDER—To melt down a solid fat. Animal fat is so treated to separate the fat from the meat tissue. This treatment is also known as "trying out" the fat.

RENNET—A natural substance extracted from the lining of the fourth stomach of calves that is used to coagulate milk in cheesemaking. Rennet extract is also used in preparing delicate milk desserts and as an ingredient in ice cream.

Refrigerator Vanilla Ice Cream

      1 **rennet tablet**
      1 **cup light cream**
   ½ **cup sugar**
   1¼ **teaspoons vanilla**
        . . .
      1 **cup whipping cream**

Crush rennet tablet in 1 tablespoon cold water; dissolve. Combine the cream and sugar; heat slowly till *warm* (110°), not hot. Stir in rennet mixture. Add vanilla; stir quickly for a few seconds. Pour into refrigerator tray. Let stand at room temperature for 10 minutes.

Freeze till firm. Break in chunks with wooden spoon; turn into chilled bowl. Beat smooth with electric mixer. Whip cream; fold into whipped mixture. Return quickly to *cold* tray; freeze firm. Makes 4 to 6 servings.

RHUBARB—A perennial plant belonging to the buckwheat family that has edible pink- to red-tinged leaf stalks and quite large, green, inedible leaves. An old-fashioned name for rhubarb is pieplant. By technical standards, rhubarb is a vegetable, but because of the ways in which it is used in cooking, homemakers usually associate rhubarb with fruits.

No one knows for sure where rhubarb originated. One theory is that it probably first grew in the southern part of Siberia, then was brought to the western world via Italy. However, Chinese writings from 2700 B.C. indicate that certain species of rhubarb have long been used for medicinal purposes in that country.

How rhubarb is produced: The rhubarb plant is very hearty and grows well in northern and southern climates. Most often, rhubarb is propagated by dividing the roots, but occasionally seeds are employed. With either method, the stalks are not ready for use until two years after they have been planted. A crop can be harvested early in the year if the plants are subjected to hothouse procedures.

Nutritional value: Raw rhubarb has very few calories (16 calories to 3½ ounces), but the caloric value soars when enough sugar is added to make the rhubarb taste good (143 calories to ⅜ cup of cooked, sweetened rhubarb). Although it is not a significant contributor of any one nutrient, rhubarb contains an assortment of important vitamins and minerals.

How to select and store: Both fresh and frozen rhubarb can be purchased. The largest share of fresh rhubarb is available between February and June.

When buying rhubarb, choose stalks that are fresh-looking, firm, bright, and glossy, and that contain a fairly large amount of pink or red color. Avoid extremely thick stems, as these will usually be tough and stringy, and wilted or flabby ones, which will lack freshness. Store rhubarb in the vegetable crisper of the refrigerator. Since it is perishable, be sure to use rhubarb within a few days.

A fluted tube mold makes Ruby Rhubarb Salad, served with tangy, whipped cream dressing, party-special. And there's a surprise inside, too—cream cheese cubes and sliced banana.

Serve generous portions of rosy Rhubarb Ice Cream by itself as shown, or add a topping of slightly sweetened and mashed strawberries.

How to prepare and use: The flavor of raw rhubarb stalks is strongly acidic, but when it is cooked and sweetened, rhubarb has a lingering tartness that is very pleasing to many people. Avoid eating the leaves, as they may be poisonous due to their high oxalic acid content. However, the stalks are perfectly safe to eat.

Rhubarb preparation is an agreeably simple operation. Cut off the leaves and the stalk ends of the rhubarb, then wash the stalks carefully in cold water. For speedier top-of-the-range or in-the-oven cooking, cube or dice the stalks.

Rhubarb Sauce, one of the easiest rhubarb recipes to make, has multiple uses. It is popularly served as a side dish, as a dessert by itself, or as a dessert topping for cake, ice cream, or pudding.

Rhubarb Sauce

> 3 cups rhubarb, cut in 1-inch pieces
> $\frac{1}{2}$ to $\frac{3}{4}$ cup sugar

In saucepan combine rhubarb, sugar, and $\frac{1}{4}$ cup water. Bring to boiling. Cover; cook over low heat till tender, 5 minutes. Makes 2 cups.

Rhubarb is often used as a pie filling. This being the case, it is easy to see why it has long been called pieplant.

Rhubarb Pie

> 1 pound rhubarb, cut in 1-inch slices (4 cups)
> 1$\frac{2}{3}$ cups sugar
> $\frac{1}{3}$ cup all-purpose flour
> Dash salt
> Pastry for 2-crust 9-inch pie (See *Pastry*)
> 2 tablespoons butter or margarine

Combine the first 4 ingredients. Let stand 15 minutes. Prepare pastry. Line 9-inch pie plate with half of pastry. Fill with rhubarb mixture. Dot with butter. Adjust the top crust, cutting slits for the escape of steam. Seal and flute. Bake at 400° for 50 minutes.

Strawberry–Rhubarb Pie

Combine 1$\frac{1}{2}$ cups sugar, 3 tablespoons quick-cooking tapioca, $\frac{1}{4}$ teaspoon salt, and $\frac{1}{4}$ teaspoon ground nutmeg. Mix in 1 pound rhubarb, cut in $\frac{1}{2}$-inch pieces, and 1 cup sliced fresh strawberries. Let stand 20 minutes.

Prepare pastry for one 9-inch lattice-top pie (See *Pastry*). Line 9-inch pie plate with pastry. Fill with fruit mixture. Dot with 1 tablespoon butter or margarine. Adjust lattice top; seal. Bake at 400° for 35 to 40 minutes.

The flavor of rhubarb stands on its own merits and also blends well with many fruits — strawberries, pineapples, bananas, and cherries. Such perky combos produce invigorating jams, salads, pies, and baked desserts. (See also *Vegetable*.)

Gingered-Rhubarb Jam

In large saucepan combine 4 cups diced fresh rhubarb, 3 cups sugar, 3 tablespoons finely snipped candied ginger, and 2 tablespoons lemon juice. Let stand till sugar is moistened by juices, 15 minutes. Cook over medium-high heat, stirring often, till thickened and clear, 12 to 15 minutes. Skim off foam; add few drops red food coloring, if desired. Ladle into hot, scalded jars; seal. Makes three ½-pints.

Ruby Rhubarb Salad

 2 cups diced fresh rhubarb
 ½ cup sugar
 ¼ cup water
 2 3-ounce packages strawberry
   flavored gelatin
1¾ cups cold water
 1 tablespoon lemon juice
 2 3-ounce packages cream cheese,
   chilled and diced
 1 banana, sliced
   Lemon-Orange Dressing

In saucepan combine rhubarb, sugar, and the ¼ cup water. Cover and cook over medium heat till rhubarb is barely tender, about 3 minutes, stirring occasionally. Cool. Drain, reserving syrup. Add enough water to syrup to make 2 cups; return to saucepan. Bring to boiling. Stir in gelatin till dissolved. Add cold water and lemon juice. Chill till partially set.

Stir rhubarb, cream cheese, and banana into gelatin mixture. Turn into 6½-cup mold. Chill till firm. To serve, unmold gelatin onto plate. Pass Lemon-Orange Dressing. Serves 8 to 10.

Lemon-Orange Dressing: In saucepan beat 1 egg. Add 1 teaspoon grated lemon peel, 1 teaspoon grated orange peel, 2 tablespoons lemon juice, and ⅓ cup sugar. Cook and stir over low heat till thickened, about 5 minutes. Cool to room temperature. Whip 1 cup whipping cream; fold into citrus mixture. Chill.

Rhubarb-Strawberry Compote

For garnish, top with a dollop of whipped cream—

 3 cups fresh rhubarb, cut in
   1-inch slices (¾ pound)
 ⅓ cup sugar
 1 cup water
       · · ·
 1 tablespoon cornstarch
   Dash salt
 ¼ cup cold water
 1 teaspoon lemon juice
   Few drops red food coloring
 2 cups fresh strawberries,
   sliced

In saucepan combine rhubarb, sugar, and water; bring to boiling. Reduce heat; simmer till almost tender, about 2 minutes. Remove from heat; drain rhubarb, reserving syrup. Add water to syrup, if necessary, to make 1¼ cups.

Combine cornstarch and salt with cold water; blend into the rhubarb-syrup mixture. Cook, stirring constantly, till thickened and bubbly. Cook 2 minutes longer. Remove from heat; cool slightly. Stir in lemon juice and food coloring. Gently stir in rhubarb and strawberries. Chill thoroughly. Makes 8 servings.

Rhubarb spiked with ginger cooks to a satisfyingly tart Gingered-Rhubarb Jam. It's perfect for fresh-from-the-oven biscuits.

Strawberry-Rhubarb Rolls

    ¾ cup sugar
    1 cup water
    2 cups sifted all-purpose flour
    1 tablespoon sugar
    3 teaspoons baking powder
    ½ teaspoon salt
    6 tablespoons butter or margarine
    ⅔ cup milk
    1 beaten egg
    1 tablespoon butter or margarine,
      melted
    1 cup sliced fresh strawberries
    2 cups finely diced rhubarb
    ⅓ cup sugar

Add ¾ cup sugar to water; simmer 5 minutes. Pour into 9x9x2-inch pan. Sift together flour, the 1 tablespoon sugar, baking powder, and salt; cut in the 6 tablespoons butter till like coarse crumbs. Mix milk and egg; add all at once, stirring just to moisten. Roll to 12x8-inch rectangle. Brush with melted butter.

Top with strawberries and rhubarb. Sprinkle with sugar. Roll jelly-roll fashion, starting at long side; seal edge. Cut in 12 slices; place atop syrup, cut side down. Bake at 450° for 25 to 30 minutes. Serve warm. Serves 12.

Flavorful juices stay in Strawberry-Rhubarb Pie when you flute the edges high. Top with vanilla ice cream for an à la mode treat.

Rhubarb Whip

This dessert is as light as a cloud—

    1 pound rhubarb, cut in 1-inch
      pieces (4 cups)
    ½ cup sugar
    ¼ cup water
    1 3-ounce package strawberry-
      flavored gelatin
    ½ cup cold water
          . . .
    ½ cup whipping cream
    Fresh strawberries, halved

In saucepan combine rhubarb, sugar, and the ¼ cup water. Bring to boiling, stirring occasionally. Cover and cook over medium-high heat 8 to 10 minutes. Add strawberry-flavored gelatin; continue to cook and stir till gelatin dissolves. Stir in the ½ cup cold water. Chill gelatin mixture till partially set.

Whip cream. With electric or rotary beater whip gelatin till fluffy; fold in cream. Spoon into sherbets; chill till serving time. Garnish with strawberries. Makes 5 to 6 servings.

Rhubarb Crunch

Best served warm—

    1 pound rhubarb, cut in 1-inch
      pieces (4 cups)
    ½ cup granulated sugar
    1 tablespoon all-purpose flour
    1 teaspoon shredded orange peel
          . . .
    ¾ cup all-purpose flour
    ¾ cup brown sugar
    Dash salt
    ¼ cup butter or margarine
    ½ cup dairy sour cream
    2 tablespoons confectioners' sugar
    ½ teaspoon vanilla

Combine rhubarb, granulated sugar, the 1 tablespoon flour, and orange peel; turn mixture into an 8¼x1¾-inch round baking dish.

For topping combine flour, brown sugar, and salt. Cut in butter till crumbly. Sprinkle over rhubarb. Bake at 350° for 40 to 45 minutes. Combine sour cream, confectioners' sugar, and vanilla; spoon atop. Serves 6.

Rhubarb Ice Cream

3 cups diced fresh rhubarb
¾ cup sugar
1 cup water
2 tablespoons lemon juice
¼ teaspoon salt
¼ teaspoon red food coloring
2 egg whites
¼ cup sugar

In saucepan combine rhubarb, the ¾ cup sugar, and water. Cook, covered, till tender, 10 to 15 minutes. Cool slightly; add lemon juice, salt, and food coloring. Pour into an 8-cup refrigerator tray; freeze till firm.

Break frozen mixture into chunks; place in *chilled* bowl and beat smooth with electric mixer. Beat egg whites till soft peaks form. Gradually add the ¼ cup sugar, beating till stiff peaks form. Whip cream; fold egg white mixture and whipped cream into rhubarb mixture. Freeze till firm. Makes ½ gallon.

Rhubarb Cake

3 tablespoons butter or margarine, melted
½ cup sugar
Few drops red food coloring
1 pound rhubarb, finely diced (about 3 cups)
1 package 1-layer-size white cake mix

Combine butter, the ½ cup sugar, and food coloring. Add rhubarb; toss mixture lightly. Spread in an 8x8x2-inch pan. Prepare cake mix using package directions; pour over fruit. Bake at 375° till done, about 35 minutes.

Immediately run spatula around edge of pan and invert onto serving plate. Before lifting off pan, let syrup drain onto cake for 3 to 5 minutes. Cut while warm. Pass whipped cream, if desired. Makes 6 to 8 servings.

RIB—A portion of a meat carcass containing rib bones and meat that make excellent eating. Meat cuts identified as rib roasts, short ribs, spareribs, and riblets are all taken from various portions of the rib section. (See also *Meat*.)

RIBBON CAKE—A novelty cake for special occasions. It takes its name from the four different-colored layers that give it a ribbon appearance when sliced.

Ribbon Cake

Prepare 1 package 1-layer-size white cake mix according to package directions; divide batter in half. To *half* add 2 drops red food coloring; leave other half white. Pour each batter into paper-lined 8x1½-inch round pan. Bake at 350° till done, 12 to 15 minutes. Cool.

Prepare 1 package 1-layer-size yellow cake mix according to package directions; divide batter in half. To *half* add one 1-ounce square unsweetened chocolate, melted and cooled, and 1 tablespoon milk. Add 5 drops yellow food coloring to other half. Pour each batter into paper-lined 8x1½-inch round pan. Bake at 350°, about 15 minutes. Cool. Fill and frost with Seven Minute Frosting. (See *Frosting*.)

RIBOFLAVIN *(rī′ bō flā′ vin)*—A water-soluble B vitamin once known as vitamin B2 and as vitamin G. Riboflavin is fairly stable to heat and acids, but it is destroyed by light or alkalies.

Although nutritional research on riboflavin began in 1879, it was not until the 1930s that its function began to be understood. Riboflavin plays a role in the proper functioning of the eyes and nervous system, and in reproduction and lactation. Riboflavin helps the cells use oxygen and combines with body proteins in the formation of important enzymes.

A riboflavin deficiency affects the corneas of the eyes and produces sores around lips and reddening and scaling of the skin around nose, ears, and mouth.

Although not stored by the body, generous amounts of riboflavin are available in many of the foods consumed daily—milk, cheese, meats (especially liver), eggs, dark green leafy vegetables, whole and enriched cereal grains, and legumes. Cooking methods that retain riboflavin best are those that use a minimum of cooking liquid, have a short cooking time, and expose a minimum of the food's surface area. (See also *Nutrition*.)

RICE—The starchy seed of a cereal grass. Rice is native to the delta areas of the major Asiatic rivers: Tigris, Euphrates, Ganges, and Yangtze. Wild rice, although often thought to be a member of the rice family, is the seed of a marsh grass.

Primitive man depended heavily on rice for survival, just as much of the world's population does today. Even before crops were cultivated or history was recorded, he gathered rice and the seeds of other wild grasses for his food.

As civilization developed and man began to keep records, surviving writings show that rice continued to play an important role in the diet. From these writings we know that around 3000 B.C., a plant called *newaree* in India was an early form of rice and that a Chinese ruler started a rice-planting feast.

The migration of rice from the Orient to the Middle East to Europe occurred via the usual method of traders or invaders introducing it to an area where it was later cultivated. For example, the Saracens took rice home with them, to what is now Europe, during medieval times.

Its arrival into the United States, however, was most unusual. In 1694 a ship bound for England from the island of Madagascar was blown off course and onto the east coast of South Carolina. It landed at Charleston, where the natives took care of the captain and his crew. In appreciation, the captain presented the governor of the colony with a handful of rough rice grains. From these grains stem the cereal crop that now is a staple of many "deep south" states. That rice is able to grow in the deep south states, extending from the Carolinas to Louisiana and Texas, is a testament of the high productivity and adaptability of this cereal.

Today, rice is a major crop in the southern rice belt (Arkansas, Louisiana, Mississippi, and Texas) and in California.

Buffet entertaining

← Use burners to keep Shrimp Elegante with Rice warm on the buffet table. Complete the menu with a bread, salad, and dessert.

However, on the world scale, the American crop is not large, as 95 percent of the world crop is grown in Asiatic countries.

How rice is produced: For best growth, rice needs temperatures that are tropical to temperate and an abundant supply of fresh water that will cover the land. The two main types of rice are aquatic, which is grown in marshy or flooded lands, and hill rice, grown where the rainfall is steady and the growing season is long.

The harvesting of rice, done primarily by man and animal power in the Orient, is a mechanized process in the United States. Tractors, threshers, and loading machinery all lighten the work of rice farmers. Airplanes are also used in seeding, fertilizing, and for pest control.

Rice is harvested with a thresher. The kernel of rice, as it leaves the thresher, is enclosed by a hull or husk and is known as paddy or rough rice. Before this rice is processed, it is mechanically dried to bring the moisture content down to about 13 to 14 percent, which is low enough to prevent the grain from spoiling while in storage. During commercial drying, a coarse cleaning removes foreign materials. After drying, the rice is either stored for use as seed or animal feed or taken to the milling and processing plant.

At the processing plant, the first step in rice milling is removing the husk from each grain of rice. After this has been done, the rice is called *brown rice.* Only a small amount is marketed in this form. Brown rice is the most nutritious of the rice forms and has a nutlike flavor and a chewy texture.

The form of rice that is most familiar to the housewife is *white milled rice,* from which several layers of bran have been removed. The process of removing the bran to reveal the familiar white rice kernel takes several steps and two or three types of machines. After the removal of the bran, the rice is ready for further optional processing or grading.

One of the optional processing steps involves adding vitamins to the grain to produce *enriched rice.* Another process that increases the nutritional value of rice is parboiling. *Parboiled rice* results from a soaking and steaming process that forces the water-soluble B vitamins from the outer layers and the germ into the center of the grain. This process also gelatinizes the starch, which produces grains that stay separate when cooked.

Precooking is a process in which the rice is cooked after milling. The moisture is then removed by dehydration. *Precooked rice* is a "convenience food" because restoring the water content takes only a few minutes of heating in water.

Nutritional value: All rice has high energy value due to the high carbohydrate content. Rice is also a source of calcium, iron, and the B vitamins (thiamine, niacin, and riboflavin). It even contributes a small amount of protein to the diet.

The different forms of rice, however, vary greatly in vitamin and mineral content. Brown rice makes the biggest nutritive contribution to the diet, followed by parboiled, enriched, and regular milled white rice. A ½-cup serving of plain cooked rice yields about 90 calories.

The low fiber content of rice makes it easy to digest, and the chemical structure of rice enables the body to use it effectively. While polished rice does lack some nutrients, the accompaniments with

To test for doneness, squeeze grains of rice between your thumb and forefinger. The rice is done if there is no hard core.

How much rice to cook

When figuring how much rice to prepare, it is helpful to know the proportion of uncooked rice to cooked rice. The following measurements will be helpful to you. Count on ½ cup of cooked rice per serving.

Uncooked	Cooked
1 cup regular milled white rice	3 cups
1 cup parboiled rice	4 cups
1 cup brown rice	3 cups
1 cup precooked rice	2 to 3 cups

which it is generally served, often meat and vegetable sauces, make up for its shortcomings. In any case, rice provides an economical source of energy.

Rice classifications: Although there are thousands of rice varieties, they are generally classified into three main groups — long-, medium-, and short-grain rice.

The grains of long-grain rice are four or five times as long as they are wide. The cooked grains are light and fluffy, and they tend to separate well. This type of rice is preferred for salads and meat dishes such as curries and stews.

Plump, fairly short kernels identify short- and medium-grain rice. When they are cooked, these types produce moist, tender rice that is easily molded, such as croquettes and rice rings.

How to buy and store: Whether you buy long-, medium-, or short-grain rice as brown rice, regular rice, parboiled rice, precooked rice, or rice mixed with seasonings depends on personal preference and on how you are going to use the rice. If the rice is to be a side dish, any kind of rice is suitable. However, if the rice is to be combined with other ingredients, use the kind specified in the recipe.

Rice usually is purchased packaged in either cardboard cartons or see-through packages. For storage, it is best to transfer rice from its package into a container with a tight lid. This will deter insect invaders. Rice keeps on the pantry shelf for up to six months, so it's easy to keep a supply of this grain on hand.

How to prepare: One of the advantages of serving rice is that it takes only a minimum of effort to prepare. Simply combine the rice, water, and seasonings, such as salt, and then cook the mixture either on top of the range or in the oven. To test the rice for doneness, pinch a grain between your fingers. It is done if there is no hard core. When preparing precooked rice or other specially processed rice, follow the label directions carefully. For flavor and color variation, brown the rice before cooking it.

Since rice combines well with so many foods, leftovers are more of a bonus than a problem. Tightly covered rice keeps in the refrigerator for up to a week and in the freezer for up to eight months. To re-heat cooked rice, put one tablespoon water per cup of rice in a saucepan, then cover and simmer until the rice is heated.

Fluffy Rice

   1 cup uncooked rice
   2 cups cold water
   ½ to 1 teaspoon salt

Put uncooked rice, water, and salt in a 2-quart saucepan; cover with a tight-fitting lid. Bring to a vigorous boil; then, turn heat as low as possible. Continue to cook for 14 minutes. Do not stir or lift cover. Remove from heat; allow rice to steam, covered, for an additional 10 minutes. Makes about 3 cups.

Browned Rice

Toast 1 cup uncooked long-grain rice in *un-greased* skillet over medium heat, shaking often, till rice is golden brown, about 20 minutes. Turn into 1-quart casserole; add 2½ cups hot water and ¼ teaspoon salt, stirring to separate rice. Cover and bake at 350° till rice is tender and all water is absorbed, about 1 hour. Fluff rice with fork. Garnish with chopped pimiento, if desired. Serves 6.

How to use: A bowlful of hot, fluffy rice is a delicious substitute for potatoes or other vegetables. Although butter alone is a popular seasoning, you can vary the flavor of rice by adding seasonings such as cumin, cinnamon, curry powder, parsley, onion, saffron, green pepper, and chives. Another easy way to flavor rice is to cook the rice in liquids such as chicken broth or tomato juice rather than in water.

Remember, however, that rice has many places in the menu other than as a side dish. For a flavorful first course try a soup containing rice. Rice also has a place in the salad course. It is delicious in vegetable, gelatin, and meat salads.

One of the most frequent uses for rice is in main dishes. A bed of hot rice is an excellent base for saucy main dishes such as beef stroganoff, chicken à la king, and pork chow mein. To make the main course fancier, mold the hot rice into a ring shape. Casseroles are another popular use for rice. It's easy to make an enticing casserole with rice and any of a variety of meats, seafoods, and vegetables.

Rice is even used in desserts. Custardy rice pudding is probably the most popular dessert made with rice, but rice is also used in various other puddings, and in fruit dessert recipes. (See also *Grain.*)

Delight guests with tasty Rice and Tuna Pie, which uses a subtly herbed rice shell as the base for the tuna, egg, and cheese filling.

Confetti Rice Ring

Cook one 10-ounce package frozen peas according to package directions; drain. Combine 4 cups hot cooked rice, peas, 3 tablespoons chopped canned pimiento, and 2 tablespoons butter or margarine, melted. Press lightly into greased 5½-cup ring mold. Unmold at once.

Butter-Baked Rice

     1 cup parboiled rice
       Dash garlic salt
    ¼ cup butter or margarine
     1 13¾-ounce can chicken broth
       or 2 chicken bouillon cubes
       dissolved in 1¾ cups boiling
       water
     2 tablespoons finely snipped
       parsley
    ¼ cup toasted, slivered
       almonds (optional)

Place uncooked rice in 1-quart casserole; sprinkle with ¼ teaspoon salt and garlic salt. Add butter and hot bouillon; stir to combine. Cover tightly. Bake at 325° for 35 minutes. Stir occasionally. Remove cover. Stir in parsley. Sprinkle with almonds, if desired. Bake, uncovered, 10 minutes longer. Makes 6 servings.

For an unusual vegetable dish, serve Green Rice Bake. This tasty blend of rice, spinach, and cheese goes well with most meats.

Green Rice Bake

In mixing bowl combine 2 slightly beaten eggs and 2 cups milk. Add ¾ cup uncooked packaged precooked rice; ⅓ cup finely chopped onion; one 10-ounce package frozen chopped spinach, cooked and drained; 4 ounces sharp process American cheese, shredded (1 cup); and ½ teaspoon garlic salt. Pour into a 10x6x 1¾-inch baking dish. Bake at 325° till firm, about 35 to 40 minutes. Makes 4 to 6 servings.

Shrimp Elegante with Rice

     3 pounds fresh or frozen shrimp
       in shells (50 large)
       Boiling water
     2 7-ounce packages frozen Chinese
       pea pods
     3 chicken bouillon cubes
    2½ cups boiling water
    ½ cup chopped green onion
     3 tablespoons soy sauce
     1 teaspoon salt
     4 tablespoons cornstarch
    ¼ cup cold water
     4 medium tomatoes, cut into
       eighths
       Saucepan Rice

Thaw shrimp, if frozen; peel and devein. Set aside. Pour boiling water over pea pods and carefully break apart with fork; drain immediately. In large saucepan or Dutch oven dissolve bouillon cubes in 2½ cups boiling water; add shrimp, onion, soy sauce, and salt. Return to boiling; cook, uncovered, for 3 minutes, stirring the shrimp mixture occasionally.

In small bowl blend together cornstarch and cold water; stir into shrimp mixture. Cook, stirring constantly, till mixture thickens and bubbles. Add tomato wedges and drained pea pods. Cook the mixture till the tomatoes are heated through, about 3 minutes longer. Spoon over hot Saucepan Rice. Makes 12 servings.

Saucepan Rice: In a large saucepan combine 2 cups uncooked long-grain rice, 4 cups cold water, and 1 teaspoon salt; cover the mixture tightly. Bring to a vigorous boil, then turn heat low. Continue cooking 14 minutes (do not lift cover). Remove from heat; let rice stand, covered, for 10 minutes. Garnish cooked rice with parsley sprigs, if desired.

Rice and Tuna Pie

    2 cups cooked rice
    2 tablespoons butter or margarine,
        melted
    1 tablespoon chopped onion
    ¼ teaspoon dried marjoram leaves,
        crushed
    1 slightly beaten egg
    1 9-ounce can tuna, drained and
        flaked
    3 beaten eggs
    1 cup milk
    4 ounces process Swiss cheese,
        shredded (1 cup)
    1 tablespoon chopped onion
    ¼ teaspoon salt
      Dash pepper
    ¼ teaspoon dried marjoram leaves,
        crushed
      Canned pimiento (optional)

For rice shell, combine cooked rice, melted butter or margarine, the 1 tablespoon chopped onion, ¼ teaspoon crushed marjoram, and 1 slightly beaten egg. Press into bottom and sides of a lightly buttered 10-inch pie plate or a 10x6x1¾-inch baking dish. Layer flaked tuna evenly over rice shell.

Combine 3 beaten eggs, milk, shredded cheese, 1 tablespoon chopped onion, salt, pepper, and dried marjoram. Pour over tuna.

Bake at 350° till knife inserted just off-center comes out clean, about 50 to 55 minutes. Garnish with pimiento, if desired. Serves 6.

Pork Chops on Amber Rice

    6 pork chops, ¾ inch thick
      Salt
      Pepper
    1⅓ cups packaged precooked rice
    1 cup orange juice
    1 10½-ounce can condensed
        chicken-rice soup

Brown pork chops in heavy skillet; season with salt and pepper. Place uncooked rice in an 11¾x7½x1¾-inch baking dish; pour orange juice over rice. Arrange browned pork chops on rice. Pour condensed chicken-rice soup over all. Cover; bake at 350° for 45 minutes. Uncover and bake 10 minutes longer. Serves 6.

Calico Rice Salad

    3 cups cooked rice
    6 hard-cooked eggs, coarsely
        chopped
    ½ cup chopped onion
    ¼ cup chopped canned pimiento
    ¼ cup chopped green pepper
    ¼ cup chopped celery
    ¼ cup chopped dill pickle
    ⅓ cup mayonnaise or salad
        dressing
    ¼ cup French salad dressing
    2 tablespoons prepared mustard
      Lettuce

Combine cooked rice, eggs, onion, pimiento, green pepper, celery, dill pickle, 1 teaspoon salt, and dash pepper. Blend together mayonnaise, French salad dressing, and prepared mustard; add to rice mixture and toss. Chill thoroughly. Lightly pack rice mixture into five 5-ounce custard cups; immediately turn out on lettuce-lined plates. Makes 5 servings.

Baked Rice Pudding

Combine 2 cups milk, 3 slightly beaten eggs, ½ cup sugar, 1 teaspoon vanilla, and ½ teaspoon salt; mix well. Add 1¾ to 2 cups cooked long-grain rice and ⅓ to ½ cup raisins (optional). Turn into 10x6x1¾-inch baking dish. Bake, uncovered, at 325° for 30 minutes; stir. Sprinkle with ground nutmeg. Continue baking till knife inserted halfway between center and edge of dish comes out clean, about 30 minutes more. Makes 6 servings.

Saucepan Rice Pudding

In a 2-quart saucepan combine 2½ cups milk, ⅔ cup uncooked packaged precooked rice, ⅓ cup sugar, 1 teaspoon vanilla, ½ teaspoon salt, and ⅓ cup raisins (optional). Bring just to boiling. Reduce heat and cook, uncovered, over low heat 20 minutes, stirring often.

Combine 1 slightly beaten egg and 2 tablespoons milk. Stir a small amount of hot rice mixture into egg; return to saucepan. Cook and stir over low heat till mixture thickens slightly, about 3 to 4 minutes. Serve warm or chilled with light cream. Makes 4 servings.

For pudding with a difference, serve Rice Pudding Royale. Coriander, fruit peel, and cottage cheese are the unusual ingredients.

Rice Pudding Royale

    3 cups milk
   ½ cup long-grain rice
   ½ cup sugar
   ¼ teaspoon salt
   ½ teaspoon grated lemon peel
   ¼ teaspoon grated orange peel
   ½ teaspoon ground coriander
   1 teaspoon vanilla
   ¾ cup cream-style cottage
      cheese

Scald milk in top of double boiler. Add uncooked rice, sugar, and salt. Cook, covered, over boiling water for 1 hour, stirring frequently. Uncover; cook till thickened, 30 to 40 minutes. Remove from heat; stir in lemon and orange peels, coriander, and vanilla. Chill.

    Beat cottage cheese; stir into rice mixture. Spoon into dessert dishes. Garnish with a little shredded orange peel or ground coriander, if desired. Makes 6 to 8 servings.

Rice Pudding

  2½ cups milk
   ½ cup long-grain rice
   ⅓ cup sugar
   ⅓ cup raisins (optional)
   1 teaspoon vanilla

In a heavy 1½-quart saucepan combine milk, uncooked rice, sugar, raisins (if desired), vanilla, and ½ teaspoon salt. Bring to boiling. Reduce heat and cook, covered, over very low heat till rice is tender and milk is absorbed, about 45 to 50 minutes; stir frequently. Serve with light cream. Makes 4 servings.

Glorified Rice

Drain one 8¾-ounce can crushed pineapple, reserving syrup. Combine ⅔ cup uncooked packaged precooked rice, ⅔ cup water, syrup, and ½ teaspoon salt. Stir to moisten. Bring to boil. Cover; simmer 5 minutes.

    Remove from heat; let stand 5 minutes. Add pineapple and 2 teaspoons lemon juice; cool. Stir in 1½ cups miniature marshmallows and 1 ripe banana, sliced. Whip 1 cup whipping cream. Fold cream and 2 tablespoons chopped maraschino cherries into rice mixture. Chill mixture thoroughly. Makes 8 servings.

Blueberry-Rice Bavarian

   1 envelope unflavored gelatin
     (1 tablespoon)
  ⅓ cup sugar
   1 7-ounce bottle lemon-lime
     carbonated beverage
   1 tablespoon lemon juice
  1½ cups cooked long-grain rice
   1 cup whipping cream
   2 cups fresh blueberries *or well-drained* frozen blueberries

In saucepan combine gelatin, sugar, and dash salt. Add ½ cup water. Heat and stir till gelatin dissolves; remove from heat. Cool. Stir in carbonated beverage, lemon juice, and cooked rice. Chill till partially set. Whip cream; carefully fold cream and blueberries into gelatin mixture. Spoon into sherbet glasses; chill till set. Makes 8 servings.

RICE CEREAL—Rice processed into puffed kernels, flakes, or granules for use as a breakfast cereal. (See also *Cereal.*)

Flowerpot Cookie Cups

  6 cups puffed rice cereal
  ½ pound large marshmallows (32)
  ¼ cup butter or margarine
  ¼ teaspoon peppermint flavoring
  Chocolate ice cream
  Flowers made from gumdrops
    and pipe cleaners

Place puffed rice cereal in shallow pan. Heat at 350° for 10 minutes. Turn into a large, greased bowl. Melt marshmallows and butter over very low heat, stirring till mixture is smooth; add peppermint flavoring.

Pour marshmallow mixture over cereal, mixing till all the cereal is coated. Press into bottom and sides of 10 greased custard cups. (If mixture cools too fast, return to oven and heat slightly.) Cool; remove from cups. Fill with chocolate ice cream (or a combination of your favorite flavors). Insert gumdrop flowers in ice cream. Makes 10.

Meatball Casserole

  ½ cup chopped onion
  1 tablespoon butter or margarine
  2 15¼-ounce cans meatballs in
    gravy
  1 16-ounce can sliced carrots,
    drained
  2 tablespoons snipped parsley
  2 teaspoons Worcestershire sauce
  ¼ cup crushed, crisp rice cereal
  ½ teaspoon sesame seed
  1 package refrigerated biscuits
  Milk

In large skillet cook onion in butter till tender but not brown. Add meatballs and gravy, carrots, parsley, and Worcestershire sauce. Heat till bubbling. Pour into 2-quart casserole. Mix cereal, sesame seed, and ⅛ teaspoon salt. Brush tops of biscuits with milk; then dip in cereal mixture. Arrange biscuits atop *hot* meat mixture. Bake at 425° till biscuits are done, 10 to 12 minutes. Serves 6.

Creamy white ricotta cheese has a nutlike flavor.

Eggs Au Gratin

In skillet melt 2 tablespoons butter or margarine. Add 2 cups crisp rice cereal and mix gently. Spoon *half* the cereal mixture into bottoms of four 10-ounce casseroles.

In saucepan combine one 11-ounce can condensed Cheddar cheese soup, ¼ cup milk, and ¼ cup sliced ripe olives; heat through. Slice 6 hard-cooked eggs (reserve 8 slices for garnish). Fold eggs into soup mixture. Spoon into prepared casseroles. Top each with 2 egg slices; wreathe with remaining cereal. Bake at 400° about 15 minutes. Makes 4 servings.

RICE FLOUR—Finely milled flour that is made from white rice. This flour is used most frequently as a substitute for all-purpose flour in wheat-free diets.

RICER—A kitchen utensil that consists of a perforated cylinder and a plunger. Foods, such as cooked potatoes, are placed in the cylinder and then forced through the holes by the plunger. This gives particles that resemble grains of rice.

RICOTTA CHEESE (*ri kot'uh, -kô'tuh*)—A creamy smooth, almost satiny, uncured cheese traditionally made from the whey left from the manufacture of other cheeses. Ricotta, first made in Italy and still very popular in Europe, resembles cottage cheese in appearance and flavor.

Although European ricotta is made almost exclusively from whey, that of the United States is usually made from whole milk or a mixture of whey and whole milk. This cheese is an ingredient in many Italian dishes. (See also *Cheese.*)

Cheese-Filled Manicotti

¾ pound ground beef
¼ pound fresh pork sausage
2 6-ounce cans tomato paste
½ cup chopped onion
1 3-ounce can sliced mushrooms, drained
2 teaspoons dried oregano leaves, crushed
1 teaspoon sugar
1 large clove garlic, minced
1½ cups ricotta *or* cream-style cottage cheese, drained
¼ cup Parmesan cheese
1 slightly beaten egg
2 tablespoons snipped parsley
6 to 8 manicotti

In large saucepan brown meats; drain off excess fat. Add 2 cups water, tomato paste, onion, mushrooms, oregano, 1½ teaspoons salt, sugar, and garlic. Simmer, uncovered, for 30 minutes, stirring occasionally. Meanwhile, combine ricotta *or* cottage cheese, Parmesan cheese, egg, parsley, and ½ teaspoon salt.

Cook manicotti in boiling salted water just till tender, about 20 minutes; drain. Rinse in cold water; drain. Using small spoon, stuff each shell with about 3 tablespoons cheese mixture. Pour *half* the meat sauce into 11¾x7½x1¾-inch baking dish. Arrange stuffed manicotti in a row. Spoon remaining sauce over. Bake, covered, at 350° for 30 to 35 minutes. Pass Parmesan, if desired. Serves 4 to 6.

Blonde Lasagne

Cook 3 ounces wide noodles (2⅓ cups) in boiling, salted water till tender; drain. Cook one 10-ounce package frozen peas according to package directions; drain. Cook 12 slices bacon till crisp; drain and crumble. Tear 6 ounces provolone cheese into pieces. In greased 10x6x1¾-inch baking dish, arrange *half* the noodles; top with bacon, 1 cup ricotta or cream-style cottage cheese, peas, *half* the provolone cheese, and *half* of a 10½-ounce can white sauce. Top with remaining noodles, remaining provolone cheese, and remaining white sauce.

Combine 1 cup bread crumbs and 2 tablespoons butter, melted; sprinkle over casserole. Bake at 350° for 25 minutes. Serves 4 or 5.

Peppy Lasagne

In skillet cook 1 pound bulk Italian sausage, ½ cup chopped onion, ½ cup chopped celery, and ½ cup chopped carrot till meat is lightly browned. Drain off excess fat. Stir in one 16-ounce can tomatoes, cut up; one 6-ounce can tomato paste; 1 teaspoon salt; ½ teaspoon dried oregano leaves, crushed; and ¼ teaspoon pepper. Simmer, uncovered, for 30 minutes, stirring mixture occasionally.

Cook 10 ounces lasagne noodles according to package directions; drain well. Combine 3 cups ricotta or cream-style cottage cheese, ½ cup grated Parmesan cheese, 2 beaten eggs, 2 tablespoons parsley, and ¼ teaspoon pepper.

Place *half* the noodles in a greased 13½x8¾x1¾-inch baking dish. Spread with *half* the cheese filling; add 8 ounces mozzarella cheese, thinly sliced, and *half* the meat sauce. Repeat layers using another 8 ounces mozzarella cheese. Bake, uncovered, at 375° for 30 minutes. Let stand 10 to 15 minutes before serving. Cut into squares to serve. Serves 10 to 12.

RIGATI—A word meaning grooved that often is applied to hollow forms of pasta that have a ridged surface.

RIGATONI *(rig′ uh tō′ nē)*—A popular type of pasta that is tube-shaped and has a ridged surface. (See also *Pasta*.)

RIJSTTAFEL *(rī stä′ fuhl)*—A type of Indonesian banquet, which was adopted by the Dutch settlers and is now popular in the Netherlands as well as in Indonesia. At a typical presentation, many dishes are served by a steady stream of waiters.

As is indicated by the word rijsttafel, which literally means rice table, rice is an important part of this meal. Traditionally, rice is placed in the center of the guest's plate, and around it is heaped a selection of food from a large assortment of dishes. This array often includes pork, chicken, duck, goose, beef, lamb, fish, crab, shrimp, lobster, vegetables, and fruits prepared in various ways.

Although the size of a traditional rijsttafel limits it to special restaurants, you can serve a mini-rijsttafel to your guests by using the following recipes.

Rijsttafel Rice

1½ cups long-grain rice
2¼ cups cold water

Wash uncooked rice 3 to 4 times alternately in cold and warm water. Soak the rice 15 minutes in cold water; then drain. Add rice to the 2¼ cups cold water; bring to a boil. Stir once. Then, cover the kettle tightly and turn heat down as low as possible. Cook rice for 15 minutes without removing the cover.

Lift cover and test rice for doneness, but do not stir it. If the rice is not sufficiently cooked, sprinkle a little hot water over it. Replace the cover and steam for 3 to 5 minutes longer. Turn off heat and let kettle of rice stand for 5 minutes. Serve cooked rice without stirring. It should be soft, yet grainy, fluffy, and entirely dry. Any small amount of rice that adheres to the kettle should be discarded rather than used. Serve the hot rice with Pork Sate and Peanut Sauce. Makes 8 servings.

Pork Sate (Pork Kabobs)

Use the blender to mix the marinade—

3 cups onion pieces
¼ cup peanut butter
1 clove garlic
3 tablespoons soy sauce
1 tablespoon brown sugar
1½ teaspoons ground coriander
1½ teaspoons salt
1 teaspoon grated lemon peel
1½ teaspoons lemon juice
1 teaspoon ground cumin
½ teaspoon ground red pepper
½ teaspoon black pepper
2 pounds boneless lean pork,
    cut in ¾-inch cubes

In blender container combine onion, peanut butter, garlic, soy sauce, brown sugar, coriander, salt, lemon peel, lemon juice, cumin, red pepper, and black pepper. Cover and blend for 30 seconds. Marinate pork cubes in this mixture overnight in the refrigerator.

Thread pork cubes on skewers and broil 3 to 4 inches from heat till pork is cooked through and very tender, about 15 to 18 minutes, turning once. Makes 8 servings.

Peanut Sauce

In a saucepan combine ½ cup coconut milk (milk drained from fresh coconut, with water added, if necessary, to make ½ cup liquid), 2 tablespoons peanut butter, 1 tablespoon minced green pepper, 1½ teaspoons lemon juice, 1 teaspoon brown sugar, and 1 teaspoon soy sauce. Simmer over low heat for 5 minutes. Use as a dip for Pork Sate. Makes ⅔ cup.

RILLETTE *(ri let)*—A French hors d'oeuvre specialty consisting of spiced or well-seasoned ground pork or pork pâté.

RIND—1. The rather thick outer coating of certain vegetables and fruits, especially citrus fruits. 2. The pig skin on smoked bacon or ham. 3. The crust on cheese.

RING MOLD—A circular mold, usually of metal, with a hole in the center. It is most commonly used for molding gelatin in the form of a ring. However, cooked rice may be pressed into a ring mold to take its shape, and spinach or carrot mixtures are sometimes baked in such a mold.

Foods molded in a ring mold are attractively served by filling the hollow center with a complementary food. For example, try fruits, vegetables, or a dressing with gelatin molds, creamed chicken or seafood with rice, and peas with carrots, diced carrots, or beets with a spinach ring.

RIPEN—To allow foods such as fruits, vegetables, and fruitcakes to attain full maturity, best texture, and richest flavor.

Fruits that must be picked before the last stage of ripeness to withstand the rigors of shipping and handling (peaches, tomatoes, and avocados, for example) or to have best eating texture (pears) often need a day or two of ripening at room temperature before they are ready to use.

To hasten the ripening of bananas and tomatoes, enclose them in a paper bag. Don't put ripening fruits on a sunny windowsill because they will wrinkle and shrivel rather than ripen properly.

RISOTTO *(ri sô′ tō, -sot′ ō)*—The Italian name for various rice dishes.

RISSOLE *(ri sōl′, ris′ ōl)*—A small, fried pastry of French origin that has a meat or a sweet filling. Rissoles are generally served as appetizers and light main dishes; however, smaller versions are used as garnishes on meat dishes.

Rissoles are shaped into small balls like fritters or folded like turnovers. They are usually fried in deep fat. However, some are panfried or ovenfried. Rissoles are served with lemon or a sauce.

RISSOLE POTATOES—Small pieces of potato cooked in the rissole manner. The potatoes are either fried in deep fat or browned in a skillet till golden and crisp.

RIVVEL—A Pennsylvania Dutch word meaning lump or flake. Rivvel soup is made by dropping a flour mixture into boiling broth. This is done by rubbing the dough through the hands, by pushing it through the holes in a colander, or by simply dropping in chunks of the dough. As the dough hits the boiling soup, it forms irregular-shaped lumps and flakes.

ROAST *(noun)*—A thick, tender cut of beef, pork, lamb, or veal. Roasts are usually cooked by dry heat in an oven or over coals. However, some roasts such as chuck are less tender and require a moist-heat cooking method such as pot-roasting.

A roast differs from a steak or a chop in thickness. Roasts are usually over two inches thick, while steaks and chops are less than two inches. Steaks and chops are often made by slicing a roast into pieces of the desired thickness.

Horseradish-Stuffed Rib Roast

Combine ¼ cup prepared horseradish and 2 cloves garlic, minced. Unroll one 5- to 6-pound rolled rib roast; spread with horseradish. Reroll roast and tie securely. Balance roast on rotisserie spit, fastening with holding forks. Rub outside of roast with additional clove of garlic. Insert meat thermometer. Attach spit and turn on motor. Roast over *medium* coals till meat thermometer registers 150° for medium-rare, about 2½ to 3 hours, or till preferred doneness. Let stand 15 minutes. Serves 10 to 12.

ROAST *(verb)*—A dry-heat method of cooking. Roasting includes cooking on a spit over a fire; embedding in coals; heating in order to brown and dry out; and baking, uncovered, in an oven.

Cooking meats over fire is probably one of the oldest methods of roasting and may even be the oldest way of cooking. The modern adaptation is rotisserie cooking.

Roast Pork Chops

  1 **cup chopped onion**
  1 **clove garlic, minced**
 ¼ **cup salad oil**
 ¾ **cup catsup**
 ⅓ **cup lemon juice**
  3 **tablespoons sugar**
  2 **tablespoons Worcestershire**
    sauce
  1 **tablespoon prepared mustard**
  2 **teaspoons salt**
 ¼ **teaspoon bottled hot pepper**
    sauce
  6 **pork rib or loin chops, 1 to 1¼**
    inches thick

Cook onion and garlic in hot oil till tender but not brown. Add 1 cup water and remaining ingredients *except* chops; simmer, uncovered, for 15 minutes. Lock chops in a spit basket. Rotate over *slow* coals till done, about 45 minutes. Baste with sauce during the last 20 minutes of cooking. Makes 6 servings.

Roasting by embedding foods in coals or ashes is another ancient procedure that is still used at cookouts. Potatoes and ears of corn are cooked in this way.

Fresh Corn on the Cob

Remove husks from fresh corn. Remove silks with stiff brush. Place each ear on a sheet of foil. Spread corn liberally with softened butter or margarine and sprinkle with salt and pepper.

Wrap foil securely around each ear of corn—don't seal seam, but fold or twist foil around ends. Place on grill and roast over *hot* coals till corn is tender, 15 to 20 minutes, turning ears frequently. Pass extra butter.

Roasting versus pot-roasting

Roasted foods are cooked without moisture; pot-roasted foods, with moisture. If pan is covered, the food wrapped in foil, or moisture added, you are pot-roasting.

Chestnuts, peanuts, and coffee beans are examples of foods that are heated to brown and dry them out. This roasting develops the flavor and color of the food.

Cooking meats in an oven is the most common type of roasting. Tender cuts of beef, veal, pork, and lamb are suitable.

When roasting meats, place the meat, fat side up, on a rack in a shallow pan. This allows the meat to baste itself and holds it up and out of the drippings. The rack also provides even heat circulation. You may season the meat any time during cooking according to personal preference. Cook the meat at about 300° to 350°.

Roasting charts give you the approximate length of cooking time. Frozen meats may be roasted, but allow extra time if not indicated on the chart. A meat thermometer inserted into the meat indicates when the exact degree of doneness is reached. Roast should rest for 15 to 20 minutes before carving. (See also *Meat.*)

Savory-Stuffed Rolled Rib Roast

A sophisticated roast that pleases the men—

>   4 ounces thinly sliced ham,
>   chopped (1 cup)
>   3 slices bacon, snipped
>   1/4 cup chopped onion
>   2 tablespoons chopped pimiento-
>   stuffed green olives
>   1 clove garlic, minced
>   1 beaten egg
>   1 4- to 5-pound rolled rib roast

Combine ham, bacon, onion, olives, garlic, and egg. Unroll roast; spread ham mixture over meat. Reroll and tie roast; place on rack in shallow roasting pan. Roast at 325° till tender, about 2½ to 3 hours. Makes 12 to 14 servings.

ROASTER—An animal, such as a chicken or a pig, that is the appropriate size for roasting. Chickens classified as roasters range between three and five pounds, and their flesh is quite tender.

Roast Chicken with Stuffing

Stuffed with sweet potato and apple for holiday or year-round menus—

>   1 17-ounce can vacuum-packed
>   sweet potatoes
>   1 medium apple, peeled, cored,
>   and diced (1 cup)
>   1/3 cup chopped onion
>   6 tablespoons butter or
>   margarine
>   •   •   •
>   1 tablespoon sugar
>   1 teaspoon salt
>   1/4 teaspoon ground nutmeg
>   2 cups soft bread cubes (about
>   2½ slices bread)
>   •   •   •
>   1 3-pound whole, ready-to-cook,
>   roasting chicken
>   Salt
>   Salad oil

Drain sweet potatoes; mash. In skillet cook apple and onion in butter till tender. Stir in the 1 tablespoon sugar, the 1 teaspoon salt, and the ¼ teaspoon nutmeg. Combine with sweet potatoes and bread cubes; mix well.

Rinse bird; pat dry. Lightly salt inside; stuff with sweet potato mixture. Truss bird and place, breast side up, on rack in shallow roasting pan. Rub skin with salad oil. (If meat thermometer is used, insert in center of inside thigh muscle, making sure bulb does not touch bone.) Roast, uncovered, at 375° for 1 hour, brushing dry areas of skin occasionally with pan drippings. Cut band of skin or string between legs and tail. Continue roasting till tender, about 15 to 30 minutes longer. (Meat thermometer should register 185°.) Serves 6.

ROASTER OVEN—An electrical appliance that cooks by roasting or baking. Roaster ovens resemble large baking pans. They include an inner, removable pan and a lid usually having a glass window. A cabinet to set the roaster oven on may be bought. Some have automatic timers.

Roaster ovens hold several dishes at a time, so you can cook a complete oven meal in them. You can also roast a turkey or cook a large dish, such as baked beans for 50 people. Roaster ovens are used as warmers, too. They keep dishes hot.

ROASTING EAR – Corn in the husks cooked on an open fire. These are placed on a rack over the fire or directly on hot coals.

ROASTING PAN – A shallow, oblong pan designed for cooking meats. Roasting pans may come with racks, handles, and lids. They are constructed of metal or glass.

ROBERT SAUCE *(rô bêr')* – A brown sauce flavored with onions and mustard. Robert sauce is named after Robert Vinot, who is credited with having developed the sauce in the seventeenth century. Today, bottles of Robert sauce are available in most supermarkets. Robert sauce goes quite well with beef, pork, and poultry.

ROB ROY – An alcoholic drink made of scotch, sweet vermouth, and bitters. Also popular is a Rob Roy made with scotch, dry vermouth, and a dash of bitters, and one in which the bitters are not added.

ROCAMBOLE *(rok' uhm bōl)* – A plant of the lily family that resembles a large garlic. Often called giant garlic, it has cloves, which are used like garlic, and leaves, which are used like chives. Rocambole is more common to Europe than to America.

ROCK – **1.** A rich drop cookie flavored with spices and filled with nuts and fruits and popularly made at Christmastime. (See also *Cookie*.) **2.** A word that is used for ice. For instance, beverages served on the rocks are poured over ice cubes.

ROCK AND RYE – An alcoholic beverage made of rye whiskey, rock candy or syrup, and lemon or orange juice. Bottles of rock and rye that include all the ingredients are available at many supermarkets.

ROCK CANDY – Large, clear, hard crystals of sugar that are stuck together. Rock candy is available in either light or dark colors. It comes in thin strings and on the ends of swizzle sticks. Rock candy is used in making various kinds of alcoholic drinks such as rock and rye.

ROCK CORNISH GAME HEN – Another name for Cornish game hen. The bird is a cross of English Cornish and White Rock breeds. Thus, the word rock is sometimes added to the name of this bird. (See also *Cornish Game Hen*.)

ROCK CRAB – A small crab found along the California and New England coasts. Rock crabs resemble Dungeness crabs, but weigh only one-third to one-half pound.

Rock crabs are sold alive. The brownish-colored meat also is available fresh cooked and canned. (See also *Crab*.)

ROCKET – A plant with a strong odor and a flavor similar to horseradish. Rocket leaves are used in Europe and in the Middle East to give sharp flavor to salads.

ROCKFISH – A food fish found on the Pacific coast from California to Alaska. There are over 50 types of rockfish including the orange, yellowtail, red, and bocaccio. Rockfish coloring ranges from a black or gray to a bright orange or red. White or pink flesh has a mild flavor.

Fresh rockfish are sold whole, dressed, and filleted. In markets outside northwestern coastal areas, frozen fillets are more commonly available. Cook rockfish as you would other fat fish by baking, broiling, frying, steaming, and boiling. Cooking increases the calorie count of this fish: a 3½-ounce uncooked portion of rockfish contains 97 calories, while a 3½-ounce serving that has been oven-steamed has about 107 calories. (See also *Fish*.)

ROCK LOBSTER TAIL – A section of the rock or spiny lobster commonly sold in American supermarkets. Unlike the true lobster, whose meat is located in the claws, the majority of the meat in a rock or spiny lobster is in the tail portion.

Rock lobster tails, ranging from tiny hors d'oeuvre size to large ones for entrées, are found in the frozen foods department of most supermarkets.

Cook lobster tails by boiling or by cutting in butterfly-style and broiling. Serve the tails hot with melted butter and lemon or chill and use in salads and casseroles. Allow about one 8-ounce tail for each person. (See also *Lobster*.)

ROCK SALT—Large, coarse crystals of salt. Rock salt is sold in large bags for freezing ice cream. The salt hastens freezing by lowering the melting point of the ice around the outside of the ice cream freezer. It helps to cool beverages when poured on the ice surrounding bottles, too.

Rock salt also acts as a conductor of heat when cooking oysters or clams on the half shell. It speeds up cooking by transferring heat so that the seafoods do not become tough by cooking slowly. In addition, rock salt helps to balance small shells. (See also *Salt*.)

Clams Casino

Use oysters another time in this appetizer—

 24 small hard-shell clams
  in shells
  Salt
  • • •
 ¼ cup butter or margarine,
  softened
 ¼ cup chopped green onion
 ¼ cup chopped green pepper
 ¼ cup finely chopped celery
  2 tablespoons chopped canned
  pimiento
  1 teaspoon lemon juice
  4 slices bacon, crisp-cooked and
  crumbled
  Rock salt

Open clams. With knife remove clams from the shells. Wash shells. Place each clam in deep half of shell. Sprinkle clams with table salt. Blend remaining ingredients. Top each clam with a scant tablespoon of mixture. Arrange half-shells on rock salt in a shallow pan. Bake at 425° for 10 to 12 minutes. Serves 8.

ROE *(rō)*—The eggs of female fish and shellfish or the milt (sperm or reproductive glands filled with sperm) of male fish. The eggs of some fish, especially the sturgeon and salmon, are made into caviar. The shellfish roe are taken from crustaceans, such as the lobster. Their roe are sometimes called coral.

Roe consist of the eggs or sperm enclosed in a membrane. The size of the membrane varies with the type of fish. Those from the shad, the one most commonly used, average about five inches long, three inches wide, and one inch thick. These are available in canned, frozen, or fresh forms in supermarkets.

There are various methods used for cooking roe—boiling, baking, and broiling. Regardless of the method used, first simmer the roe in salted or seasoned water for about 15 minutes. The membrane should be punctured before boiling so that it will not burst. After precooking, roe are used in entrées or appetizers.

Roe supply protein, B vitamins, and vitamin C in the diet. A 3½-ounce portion has 130 calories before other ingredients are added to the dish.

Fried Shad Roe

A change of pace for brunch or lunch—

  2 pairs fresh shad roe*
  2 cups water
  1 tablespoon vinegar
  1 teaspoon salt
  1 beaten egg
  1 tablespoon lemon juice
 ½ cup crushed saltine crackers
 ¼ cup butter or margarine
  Paprika

Rinse roe. In saucepan combine water, vinegar, and salt. Bring to boiling. Add roe. Cover and simmer till done, 5 to 10 minutes; drain.

Cut roe into serving-sized pieces. Combine egg and lemon juice. Dip roe into egg mixture and roll in cracker crumbs. Fry in butter till browned, turning carefully. Sprinkle roe with paprika, if desired. Makes 4 servings.

*Or substitute one 7½-ounce can shad roe and omit precooking roe in salted water.

ROLL *(noun)* — 1. A small, individual-sized bread. 2. A thin sweet bread with a jam or sweet filling that is often called a sweet roll. 3. A cut of meat that is boned and wrapped around itself.

Rolls in the first and most used sense are popular as dinner breads. Served hot from the oven, homemade rolls have an enticing aroma and flavor. They add a special, personal touch to the meal.

Making rolls for your family is similar to making breads. Rolls are usually made of yeastlike breads but consist of a richer, softer dough than breads. The basic techniques of mixing breads apply to rolls. The dough is kneaded, then allowed to rise in the bowl. The dough is proofed (rises a second time) after being shaped.

Roll recipes give the temperature and approximate length of baking time for the dough. Additional tests for doneness are the golden brown color and the hollow sound when you tap the bottom or side of a roll. Remove rolls from pan immediately and serve hot or cool on a rack.

If you do not want to mix and bake the rolls at the same time, rolls from recipes such as the following one keep well in the freezer or refrigerator. You can freeze completely or partially baked rolls (cooked 30 minutes at 350°) for two months. Partially baked rolls need to be thawed 15 minutes and baked at 450° for 5 to 10 minutes. If you plan to serve the rolls within five days, refrigerate according to the recipe for Refrigerator Rolls.

Bring out an elegant, late-evening snack of Coffeetime Twists and Cappuccino (see *Cappuccino* for recipe). The glazed hot rolls boast a filling of brown sugar and cinnamon.

Basic Roll Dough

Shape into cloverleaf, butter fan, bowknot, or Parker House rolls—

1 package active dry yeast
3½ cups sifted all-purpose flour

• • •

1¼ cups milk
¼ cup sugar
¼ cup shortening
1 teaspoon salt
1 egg

In large mixer bowl combine yeast and *2 cups* flour. Heat milk, sugar, shortening, and salt just till warm, stirring occasionally to melt shortening. Add to dry mixture in mixing bowl; add egg. Beat at low speed with electric mixer for ½ minute, scraping sides of bowl constantly. Beat 3 minutes at high speed. By hand, gradually stir in remaining flour to make a soft dough, beating well. Place in greased bowl; turn once to grease surface. Cover and let rise till double, 1½ to 2 hours.

Turn dough out on lightly floured surface and shape as desired (see page 1900 and individual entries). Cover and let rolls rise till double, 30 to 45 minutes. Bake on greased baking sheet or in greased muffin pans at 400° for 12 to 15 minutes. Makes 2 dozen rolls.

Refrigerator Rolls

Prepare Basic Roll Dough. *Do not let rise.* Place dough in greased bowl, turning once to grease surface. Cover tightly; chill at least 2 hours, or up to 4 or 5 days.

About 2 hours before serving, shape the dough as desired on floured surface. Cover; let rise till double, about 1¼ hours. Follow the baking times for Basic Roll Dough.

How to shape rolls: Using Basic Roll Dough, you can make rolls in many shapes. The most common ones are Parker House; butter fan or fantan; pan rolls; cloverleaf; bowknot and rosette; twist and corkscrew; butterhorn; and crescent or croissant.

Parker House rolls are flat circles of dough folded off-center. Butter fan or fantan rolls are made by stacking about six strips of dough and slicing these in short lengths. They are placed in a muffin tin with the cut side down. Round pan rolls are small balls of dough baked separately in muffin tins or side by side in a pan. The following recipes and pictures illustrate some of these shapes.

Manna Rolls

Onion, bacon, and beer flavor these large rolls—

2 packages active dry yeast
3¾ to 4 cups sifted all-purpose flour
¼ cup dry onion soup mix
8 slices bacon
1 12-ounce can beer (1½ cups)
¼ cup milk
1 tablespoon sugar
Melted butter or margarine
2 tablespoons yellow cornmeal

In large mixer bowl combine yeast, *1¾ cups* flour, and onion soup mix. Cook bacon till crisp; drain, reserving 2 tablespoons drippings. Crumble bacon; set aside. Heat together beer, milk, sugar, and reserved drippings just till warm (mixture will appear curdled). Add to dry ingredients in mixer bowl. Beat at low speed on electric mixer for ½ minute, scraping bowl constantly. Beat 3 minutes at high speed. Stir in crumbled bacon and enough of the remaining flour to make a moderately stiff dough.

Knead till smooth and elastic. Place in greased bowl, turning once to grease surface. Cover; let rise till almost double, 40 to 45 minutes. Punch down. Shape into 16 balls. Place in two 9x1½-inch round baking pans. Brush tops of rolls with melted butter or margarine and sprinkle with cornmeal. Cover lightly. Let rise till almost double, 25 minutes. Bake at 375° till golden, 20 minutes. Makes 16.

Cloverleaf rolls are made by placing three small balls of dough into each muffin tin. Shape balls by pulling under edges of dough.

Clothespin Rolls

> 1 package active dry yeast
> 2½ to 3 cups sifted all-purpose
>   flour
> ½ cup cornmeal
> ¾ cup milk
> ½ cup shortening
> ¼ cup sugar
> 1 teaspoon salt
> 2 eggs

In large mixer bowl combine yeast, *1½ cups* flour, and cornmeal. Heat milk, shortening, sugar, and salt just till warm, stirring occasionally to melt shortening. Add to dry ingredients in bowl; add eggs. Beat at low speed with electric mixer for ½ minute, scraping sides of bowl constantly. Beat at high speed for 3 minutes. By hand, stir in enough of the remaining flour to make a soft dough. Turn out on lightly floured surface; knead till smooth. Place in greased bowl, turning dough once to grease surface. Cover; let rise in a warm place till double, about 1¼ hours.

Punch down; turn out on lightly floured surface. Shape pieces of dough into ropes about 8 inches long and ¼ inch in diameter. Wrap around greased peg clothespins, pressing gently to seal ends. Place on greased baking sheet; cover. Let rise till double, about 45 minutes. Bake at 375° till done, about 10 minutes. Immediately remove clothespins by twisting gently. Makes 24. *Note:* Dough may be formed into 20 pan rolls. Bake 15 minutes.

Orange Rosettes

> 1 package active dry yeast
> 5 to 5½ cups sifted all-purpose
>   flour
> 1¼ cups milk
> ½ cup shortening
> ⅓ cup sugar
> 2 beaten eggs
> 2 tablespoons grated orange peel
> ¼ cup orange juice

In mixer bowl combine yeast and *3 cups* flour. Heat milk, shortening, sugar, and 1 teaspoon salt just till warm, stirring to melt shortening. Add to dry mixture; add eggs, orange peel, and juice. Beat at low speed with electric mixer ½ minute, scraping sides of bowl. Beat 3 minutes at high speed. By hand stir in enough of the remaining flour to make a soft dough.

Knead dough on lightly floured surface till smooth and elastic, about 8 to 10 minutes. Place in greased bowl, turning to grease surface. Cover; let rise in warm place till double, 2 hours. Punch down; cover and let rest 10 minutes. Roll dough in 18x10-inch rectangle, ½ inch thick. Cut strips 10 inches long and ¾ inch wide. Shape into rosettes (see picture below). Place on greased baking sheets. Cover; let rise till almost double, 45 minutes. Bake at 400° for 12 minutes. Cool on rack. Frost with Orange Icing, if desired. Makes 2 dozen.

Orange Icing: Blend 1 teaspoon grated orange peel, 2 tablespoons orange juice, and 1 cup sifted confectioners' sugar.

Bowknots are formed by rolling strips of dough lightly under fingers and tying in loose knot. Tuck under ends for rosettes.

Coffeetime Twists

1 package active dry yeast
¼ teaspoon baking soda
3 cups sifted all-purpose flour
1 cup buttermilk
3 tablespoons sugar
2 tablespoons shortening
1 teaspoon salt
1 slightly beaten egg
2 tablespoons butter, softened
⅓ cup brown sugar
1 teaspoon ground cinnamon
Icing

In mixer bowl combine yeast, soda, and *1½ cups* flour. Heat buttermilk, sugar, shortening, and salt just till warm, stirring to melt shortening. Add to dry mixture; add egg. Beat at low speed with electric mixer for ½ minute, scraping sides of bowl. Beat 3 minutes at high speed. By hand, stir in remaining flour. Turn out on lightly floured surface; knead till smooth.

Roll the dough into a 24x6-inch rectangle, about ¼ inch thick. Spread with butter. Combine brown sugar and cinnamon; sprinkle over lengthwise half of the dough. Fold other half over. Cut dough into 1-inch strips.

To form rolls, hold strip at both ends and twist in opposite directions. Place on greased baking sheet; let rise in warm place till light, about 1 hour. Bake at 375° for 12 to 15 minutes. Frost with Icing while warm. Makes 24.

Icing: Blend 1 cup confectioners' sugar, 2 tablespoons milk, and ¼ teaspoon vanilla.

Twists are made by folding dough in half and cutting into one-inch strips. Grasp each end and twist in opposite directions.

Shape butterhorns by cutting a circle of dough into wedges. Roll each wedge toward the point. Curve rolls to make crescents.

Double Butterscotch Crescents

1½ cups milk
1 4-ounce package *regular* butterscotch pudding mix
½ cup butter or margarine
2 envelopes active dry yeast
2 eggs
2 teaspoons salt
5 to 5½ cups sifted all-purpose flour
Butterscotch Filling

Using the 1½ cups milk, prepare pudding according to package directions. Remove from heat; stir in butter. Cool to lukewarm, stirring once or twice. Dissolve yeast in ½ cup warm water; stir into cooled pudding. Beat in eggs and salt. Gradually add just enough flour to make a moderately soft dough. Turn out onto floured surface and knead till dough is smooth and elastic, 5 to 10 minutes. Place in greased bowl; turn to grease surface. Let rise till double, 1 to 1½ hours. Punch down; divide into 4 parts. Cover and let rest 10 minutes.

Roll out one part of dough to a 12-inch circle. Spread with ¼ of the Butterscotch Filling. Cut into 12 triangles. Roll into crescents; place, points down, on greased baking sheet. Repeat with remaining dough and filling. Let rise till almost double, 45 minutes. Bake at 375° for 12 to 15 minutes. Cool. Makes 48.

Butterscotch Filling: Stir together ¼ cup melted butter, ⅔ cup brown sugar, ⅔ cup flaked coconut, and ⅓ cup chopped pecans.

Raisin-Cinnamon Rolls

Spread dough with a sweet filling and roll jelly-roll fashion for a pinwheel effect—

  ½ **recipe Basic Roll Dough**
  ¼ **cup granulated sugar**
  2 **tablespoons butter or margarine, melted**
  1 **teaspoon ground cinnamon**
  ¼ **cup raisins**
  1 **cup sifted confectioners' sugar**
  2 **tablespoons milk**
  ½ **teaspoon vanilla**
    Dash salt

Prepare ½ recipe Basic Roll Dough as directed, rolling dough on lightly floured surface to 16x8-inch rectangle. Combine sugar, butter, and cinnamon; spread over dough. Sprinkle with raisins. Roll lengthwise as for jelly roll. Seal edge; cut in 1-inch slices. Place, cut side down, in greased 9x9x2-inch baking pan. Cover. Let rise till double, 30 to 40 minutes.

Bake rolls at 375° till done, 20 to 25 minutes. Remove rolls from pan. Combine confectioners' sugar, milk, vanilla, and salt. Frost rolls with confectioners' icing. Makes 16.

Caramel Rolls

  ½ **recipe Basic Roll Dough**
  ¼ **cup butter or margarine, melted**
  ¼ **cup brown sugar**
  1 **teaspoon ground cinnamon**
  ½ **cup brown sugar**
  ¼ **cup butter or margarine**
  1 **tablespoon light corn syrup**

Prepare ½ recipe Basic Roll Dough as directed, rolling on lightly floured surface to 12x8-inch rectangle. Brush with ¼ cup melted butter; sprinkle with the ¼ cup brown sugar and cinnamon. Roll lengthwise as for jelly roll; seal edge. Cut roll in 1-inch slices.

In saucepan combine the ½ cup brown sugar, ¼ cup butter or margarine, and corn syrup. Heat slowly, stirring often. Pour into 8x8x2-inch baking pan. Place rolls, cut side down, over mixture. Cover; let rise in warm place till double, 35 to 45 minutes. Bake at 375° about 20 minutes. Cool 2 to 3 minutes. Invert on rack; remove pan. Makes 1 dozen rolls.

Hard Rolls

Form dough into ovals or rounds for miniature loaves of thick-crusted French bread—

Prepare ½ recipe French Bread Dough. (See *French Bread.*) Knead dough 10 to 15 minutes or till very elastic, kneading in remaining ¼ cup flour. Place dough in lightly greased bowl, turning once to grease the surface. Cover dough; let rise in warm place till double, about 45 to 60 minutes. Punch down. Let the dough rise till double again, about 30 to 45 minutes.

Turn out on lightly floured surface and divide into 2 portions. Cover and let rest 10 minutes. Divide each half into 9 portions. Shape each in oval or round roll. Place about 2 inches apart on greased baking sheets that have been sprinkled with cornmeal.

Add 1 tablespoon water to 1 slightly beaten egg white; brush over tops and sides of rolls. For crisp crusts, just brush the rolls with some water. Cover with a damp cloth, not touching dough. Let rise in warm place till double, about 45 to 60 minutes.

Place large, shallow pan on lower rack of oven; fill with boiling water. Bake rolls at 400° for 15 minutes. Brush again with egg white mixture or water. Bake till nicely browned, 10 to 15 minutes longer. For crackly crust, cool in draft. Makes 18 hard rolls.

Convenience products: If you don't have time to bake homemade rolls, look for convenience product substitutes at the supermarket. The shelves contain a wide array of brown-and-serve rolls, ready-to-serve rolls, hot roll mixes, and refrigerated rolls. These come in a variety of styles—crescent, Parker House, butter-flake, French, and pan or dinner rolls.

You can serve your family an interesting selection of breads just by using these products as they are. Or, if you want more variety, try dressing up the convenience products with additional ingredients. Spread rolls with a blend of softened butter and an herb, such as thyme, dill, sage, or basil. Cheese spreads, bits of crisp bacon, onion, and garlic also add flavor to the rolls, which, in turn, complement the entire meal and arouse the family's interest. (See also *Bread.*)

Add fragrant, orange-flavored rolls to the brunch menu to make a hit with the crowd. Make either rosettes or bowknots (shown here) from the Orange Rosette dough — the only difference is tucking under the loose ends of the knots for rosettes.

Croissants Elegante

  1 13¾-ounce package hot roll mix
  ¾ cup warm water
  1 egg
  1 tablespoon sugar
  ¾ cup *cold* butter or margarine

In large bowl dissolve yeast from hot roll mix in warm water. Stir in egg and sugar. Add roll mix; beat well. Turn out onto lightly floured surface; knead till smooth, about 3 to 5 minutes. Let dough rest for 20 minutes.

Roll *cold* butter between two sheets of waxed paper to 9x7-inch rectangle; chill. Roll dough out to 16x10-inch rectangle. Place butter rectangle on one end of dough; fold other end of dough over and seal edges. Roll dough out to a 16x10-inch rectangle; fold in thirds. Wrap in waxed paper; chill 20 minutes. Roll, fold, and chill 2 more times. After final chilling, roll chilled dough out to 20x16-inch rectangle.

Cut crosswise into 4 strips; cut each strip crosswise into 4 rectangles. Cut each rectangle diagonally into 2 triangles. Starting with long side, roll each piece of dough toward point.

Place, point down, on *ungreased* baking sheet; curve ends to form crescent. Let rise in warm place till light, about 30 to 45 minutes. Bake at 400° till the rolls are golden brown, about 12 to 15 minutes. Makes 32 rolls.

Thyme-Buttered Crescents

Try the herb butter on English muffins, too—

  ½ cup butter or margarine,
       softened
  1 teaspoon lemon juice
  ½ teaspoon dried thyme leaves,
       crushed
             • • •
  1 package refrigerated crescent
       rolls (8 rolls)

Cream butter or margarine till fluffy. Stir in lemon juice and thyme. Keep herb butter at room temperature for 1 hour to mellow before using. Unroll crescents; spread *2 teaspoons* herb butter on each crescent. Roll up and bake according to package directions. Makes 8 rolls.

ROLL *(verb)* — **1.** To coat with crumbs or chopped nuts by moving the food around in a dish of the pieces. **2.** To shape food.

Foods are rolled into many different shapes. Doughs are spread out flat with a rolling pin; jelly rolls are rolled into long, round shapes; refrigerated cookie doughs are formed into long cylinders; various mixtures are shaped into balls.

ROLLED COOKIE — A type of cookie that is spread flat and cut into shapes before baking. Rolled cookies are made from stiff doughs. If the dough is rolled very thin, the cookies will be crisp; if the dough is thicker, they will be soft.

Rolled cookies serve a dual purpose when there are children in the house. Not only are the cookies good to eat, but they are also fun to shape. Children enjoy cutting rolled cookies into designs ranging from simple triangles cut with a knife to elaborate ones made with cookie cutters. You can experiment with additional decorations by topping with sugar, small decorative candies, or icings.

Another decorative variation is to stack two cookies with or without a filling between them. Attractive combinations of colors and shapes carry out a holiday or party theme. The following recipes might be varied to suit the occasion.

Be creative with rolled cookies — it's not complicated. Try cutting tiny holes off-center with a thimble for an unusual design.

Delight children and adults with this pair of cookies. The center cutout for Cameo Cutouts (left) is made with hors d'oeuvre cutters. Mincemeat Marvels (right) are decorated with a glacé candy apple topknot.

Mincemeat Marvels

    1⅓ cups shortening
    1½ cups sugar
     2 eggs
     1 teaspoon vanilla
     1 teaspoon grated orange peel
     4 cups sifted all-purpose flour
     3 teaspoons baking powder
    ½ teaspoon salt
     2 to 3 tablespoons milk
        Mincemeat Filling

Thoroughly cream shortening, sugar, eggs, and vanilla. Stir in orange peel. Sift together flour, baking powder, and salt. Add to creamed mixture alternately with milk. Divide dough in half; chill. On lightly floured surface, roll to ⅛-inch thickness. Cut with 2¾-inch round cutter. Make small round cutout in centers of *half* the cookies.

Place 1 heaping teaspoon Mincemeat Filling on each plain cookie; top with a cutout cookie. Press edges with fork or tip of hook-type opener to seal. Place on greased cookie sheet; bake at 375° for 12 minutes. Garnish with Glacé Candy Apples, if desired. Makes 30.

Mincemeat Filling: Break one 9-ounce package mincemeat into pieces. Add 2 tablespoons sugar, 2 teaspoons grated orange peel, 1 teaspoon grated lemon peel, ½ cup orange juice, and ¼ cup lemon juice. Heat, stirring till mincemeat pieces are broken; simmer 1 minute. Cool; stir in ¼ cup chopped walnuts.

Cameo Cutouts

 ¾ cup butter or margarine
 ⅔ cup sugar
 ½ cup dark corn syrup
 1 egg
 1½ teaspoons vanilla
 3 cups sifted all-purpose flour
 1 teaspoon baking powder
 ½ teaspoon salt
 1 1-ounce square unsweetened
   chocolate, melted and cooled

Cream butter, sugar, and syrup till fluffy. Beat in egg and vanilla. Sift together flour, baking powder, and salt; stir into creamed mixture. Divide dough in half. To one half add melted chocolate; blend. Leave other half plain. Chill both doughs thoroughly.

On well-floured surface, roll chocolate dough to ⅛-inch thickness. (Keep plain dough chilled.) Cut in 2½-inch scalloped rounds. Place on *ungreased* cookie sheet. Repeat with vanilla dough. With floured tiny cutter or thimble, make center cutouts. Place chocolate cutouts on plain cookies and vice versa. Bake at 350° for 8 to 10 minutes. Cool slightly; remove the cookies to rack.

Nut-Butter Rounds

 1 cup sifted all-purpose flour
 ⅓ cup granulated sugar
 ½ cup ground pecans
 ½ cup butter or margarine, softened
 ⅔ cup sifted confectioners' sugar
 ¼ cup butter or margarine
 2 1-ounce squares unsweetened
   chocolate, melted and cooled
 Apricot preserves

Sift together flour and granulated sugar; stir in ground pecans. Blend in the ½ cup butter or margarine with spoon. On floured surface, roll to ⅛-inch thickness. Cut in 2-inch rounds and place on *ungreased* cookie sheet. Bake at 375° till lightly browned, 8 to 10 minutes. Cool slightly before removing to rack.

Cream confectioners' sugar, ¼ cup butter, and melted chocolate till well combined. Spread chocolate filling on *half* the cookies. Top chocolate-covered cookies with plain cookies. Spread tops lightly with preserves. Makes 1½ dozen.

Refrigerator cookies are a slightly different kind of rolled cookie. These are shaped into long, round cylinders and then sliced. (See also *Cookie.*)

Sugar-Pecan Crisps

 ¾ cup butter or margarine
 ⅔ cup sugar
 1 egg
 1 teaspoon vanilla
 ¼ teaspoon salt
 1¾ cups sifted all-purpose flour
 ½ cup finely chopped pecans

Cream together butter or margarine and sugar till light. Beat in egg, vanilla, and salt. Gradually stir in flour. Shape dough into 2 rolls, each about 6 inches long and 1½ inches in diameter; roll each in ¼ cup of the pecans to coat outside. Wrap in waxed paper; chill thoroughly. Cut into slices ¼ inch thick. Place on *ungreased* cookie sheet. Bake at 350° for 15 to 17 minutes. Makes 4 dozen cookies.

ROLLED OATS—A cereal product that is made by pressing oat grains into flat flakes. Rolled oats are often called oatmeal. (See also *Oatmeal.*)

Oatmeal Crunchies

 1 cup sifted all-purpose flour
 ½ cup granulated sugar
 ½ teaspoon baking powder
 ½ teaspoon baking soda
 ¼ teaspoon salt
 ½ cup brown sugar
 ½ cup shortening
 1 egg
 ¼ teaspoon vanilla
 ¾ cup quick-cooking rolled oats
 ¼ cup chopped walnuts

Sift together first 5 ingredients. Add the ½ cup brown sugar, shortening, egg, and vanilla; beat well. Stir in rolled oats and walnuts. Form into small balls. Dip tops in a little additional granulated sugar. Place on *ungreased* cookie sheet. Bake at 375° for about 10 to 12 minutes. Makes about 3½ dozen.

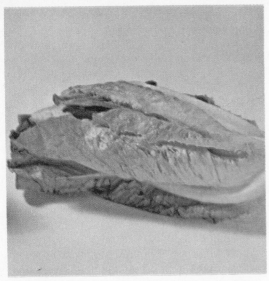

The rich green color of romaine makes a pleasing contrast in a salad greens mixture. The elongated heads and leaves are easily recognizable at the supermarket when compared to other heading lettuce varieties.

Romaine leaves are prepared in the French style by cutting out the leaf ribs with a knife. For a garnish, snip the edges of the leaves into points. Then, insert them, pointed ends out, around the salad.

ROLLING PIN—A cylindrical roller, usually with handles, used to flatten dough for pastries, cookies, and biscuits.

When rolling dough, take care not to pinch dough at the edges. Roll with even pressure, from center outward. Lift the rolling pin when it reaches the edge.

ROLLMOP—A herring fillet rolled around a piece of pickle or small onion and marinated in a seasoned, white wine solution.

ROLY-POLY—A dessert of sweet biscuit dough spread with jam or fruit filling and folded up like a jelly roll. Roly-poly can be baked, steamed, or boiled.

ROMAINE—Also called cos, this lettuce variety has a pronounced cylindrical head shape. Its coarse, dark green leaves, stronger in flavor than iceberg lettuce, overlap closely around the heart.

As is indicative of dark green vegetables, romaine is higher in vitamin A than the lighter lettuce varieties. Nonetheless, romaine is low in calories like other members of the lettuce family.

Fresh-looking, crisp romaine leaves with a minimum of blemishes should be selected. Wrapped in foil, cellophane, or a plastic bag, romaine can be stored in a vegetable crisper for up to one week.

Although much depends on other flavorings in a recipe, romaine is usually utilized with a mixture of greens. However, some classic recipes, like Caesar salad, use romaine as the only green. Stronger seasonings mute the bitter romaine flavor. (See also *Lettuce*.)

Modern Caesar Salad

Shake together ½ cup salad oil; ¼ cup red wine vinegar; 1 large clove garlic, crushed; 2 teaspoons Worcestershire sauce; ¼ teaspoon salt; and dash pepper in screw-top jar. Refrigerate a few hours or overnight to blend flavors.

Toast 3 slices bread, cubed, slowly at 225° for 2 hours. To serve, sprinkle ½ cup shredded Parmesan cheese and 1 ounce blue cheese, crumbled (¼ cup), over 8 cups torn romaine (about 1 medium head). Shake 1 egg well with dressing; toss lightly with salad. Serves 6 to 8.

ROMANO CHEESE—A very hard Italian cheese with sharp, pungent flavor and solid, granular texture. Most romano cheese is made in various regions of Italy, although some is made in America.

When first produced in Latium, Italy, romano was made solely from ewe's milk, but in recent years, cow's and goat's milk have been utilized. The milk is partly skimmed and may be pasteurized. After processing, the cheese is cured for at least five months, and, in most cases, for over one year. If short-term cured (five to eight months), romano may be eaten as a table cheese. Longer curing increases the cheese's hardness, making it suitable for grating only. Grated cheese is used with soups, spaghetti, and other dishes.

Romano is often named according to the type of milk from which it is made. When ewe's milk is used, it is called Pecorino romano; when cow's milk, Vacchino romano; when goat's milk, Caprino romano.

Since most romano available in the United States has a long-term cure, the cheese is shredded or grated and used in cooking like Parmesan cheese. Its flavor, however, is stronger than Parmesan. Thus, use it sparingly. Add a little and then increase until of the desired flavor level.

Hard romano cheese is just right for grating.

Noodles Romano

Combine ¼ cup softened butter; 2 tablespoons parsley flakes; and 1 teaspoon dried basil leaves, crushed. Blend in one 8-ounce package softened cream cheese and dash pepper; stir in ⅔ cup boiling water. Blend well. Keep warm.

Cook one 8-ounce package fettucini, thin noodles, *or* spaghetti in large amount of boiling, salted water till tender; drain. Cook 1 clove garlic, minced, in ¼ cup butter for 1 to 2 minutes; pour over noodles. Toss lightly. Sprinkle with ½ cup shredded or grated romano cheese; toss again. Pile noodles on warm platter; spoon sauce over. Sprinkle with ¼ cup shredded or grated romano cheese. Toss lightly. Garnish with parsley. Makes 6 servings.

The robust flavor of romano cheese stars in this Italian-style Noodles Romano. A smooth, cream cheese sauce moistens the thin fettucini, while fluffy parsley sprigs serve as garnish.

ROME BEAUTY APPLE—A firm, mild-flavored apple variety that is most often used for cooking and baking. (See also *Apple*.)

ROOT BEER—A nonalcoholic, caramel-colored, carbonated beverage. This sweetened, yeast-flavored drink is made with a syrup of herb, bark, and root juices.

Root beer, a popular soft drink, is sold in bottles and in jugs. If you are so inclined, you can make your own root beer. (See also *Carbonated Beverage*.)

ROQUEFORT CHEESE *(rōk′ fuhrt)*—A cheese made in Roquefort, France. Roquefort is a semisoft to hard cheese with a chalky white color and blue veins. It is made of sheep's milk.

This gourmet cheese has been made for centuries. Supposedly, it was first made by a shepherd boy who left his lunch, including curds, in a cave. When he returned sometime later, the curds had changed. Of course, his curiosity demanded that he sample this blue-streaked wonder. Whether or not this story is true is not known, but Roquefort cheese has achieved a kingly status since that time.

Today, there is a worldwide demand for this sharp, piquant cheese. However, Roquefort cannot be made any place other than in Roquefort, France. Only cheeses ripened in Roquefort caves can be labeled Roquefort and identified by the red sheep emblem on the package. There are regional dairies in France that begin the processing of the ewe's milk. Then, the curds are sent to Roquefort to be ripened in the caves. These caves have a special mold and atmospheric conditions that produce the flavor of Roquefort.

Blue, Gorgonzola, and Stilton are kin to Roquefort.

You can find Roquefort in most American supermarkets and cheese stores. How you use it will depend on your particular preference. Cheese lovers enjoy Roquefort in many types of dishes. One of the most popular uses is in salad dressing.

Roquefort Dressing

½ cup mayonnaise
½ cup light cream
1½ teaspoons lemon juice
4 ounces Roquefort cheese (1 cup)

Combine mayonnaise, light cream, and lemon juice. Crumble cheese into mayonnaise mixture; mix well. Chill. Serve with lettuce or tomato wedges, as desired. Makes 1½ cups.

Other uses for Roquefort range from appetizers of dips, canapés, and spreads to accents in meat dishes to desserts.

Roquefort Dessert Spread

8 ounces Roquefort cheese (2 cups)
1 tablespoon sauterne
3 tablespoons diced almonds, toasted
Fresh fruit

With electric or rotary beater, whip together cheese and sauterne till light and fluffy. Stir in almonds. Form mixture into a bar; chill. Slice and serve with fresh fruit.

Besides adding interesting flavor, Roquefort contributes nutrients to the diet. It contains protein, fat, calcium, phosphorus, the B vitamins, and some vitamin A. A one-ounce serving has about 110 calories. (See also *Cheese*.)

ROSÉ *(rō zā′)*—A pink table wine. Rosé is made in most wine-producing countries from black or red grapes. After a few days of fermenting, the grapes' skins are removed to control the wine's delicate color. Rosé ranges from dry to sweet and is served well chilled, about 45° to 50°. This light-bodied wine goes with most foods, especially chicken, seafood, veal, and lamb. (See also *Wines and Spirits.*)

ROSEFISH — A bright red or reddish orange, saltwater fish. The rosefish is also called redfish, blackbelly rosefish, and ocean perch. It inhabits deep waters of the northern Atlantic Ocean. The firm, rich-flavored rosefish is prepared like other fat fish. (See also *Perch.*)

ROSE GERANIUM — A fragrant member of the geranium family. The narrow, light green leaves are used in cooking.

Fresh leaves are used to give flavor to jam or jelly and to baked custards. They also make an attractive, sweetly aromatic garnish for fruit cups, fruit salads, and cakes. Dried rose geranium leaves are included in some herb-tea mixtures.

Most homemakers who like to use rose geranium leaves grow them at home, but you can get them at greenhouses and specialty food stores. (See also *Herb.*)

Rose Geranium Cake

    24 fresh rose geranium leaves
     1 cup butter or margarine
         (2 sticks)
 1¾ cups sugar
     6 egg whites
     3 cups sifted cake flour
     4 teaspoons baking powder
 ½ teaspoon salt
 ¾ cup milk
 ½ cup water
     1 teaspoon vanilla
       Rose Geranium Frosting (See
           page 1910)
       Frosted Rose Geranium Leaves
           (See page 1910)

Rinse rose geranium leaves; wrap 5 or 6 leaves around each stick of butter. Wrap butter in foil or plastic wrap; refrigerate overnight. Remove leaves; rinse and save leaves.

Cream butter; gradually add sugar, creaming till light and fluffy. Add egg whites, two at a time, beating well after each addition. Sift together flour, baking powder, and salt. Combine milk, water, and vanilla.

Alternately add dry ingredients and milk mixture to creamed mixture, beginning and ending with dry ingredients; beat smooth after each addition. Grease and flour two 9x1½-inch layer cake pans. Arrange 10 to 12 rose geranium leaves (including those saved from the butter) on bottom of each cake pan. Spoon batter over leaves. Bake at 350° till cake tests done, about 30 to 35 minutes. Cool in pans for 10 minutes. Remove cake layers from pans; cool on racks. Remove rose geranium leaves from cake bottoms; discard leaves. Frost cooled cake with Rose Geranium Frosting and garnish with Frosted Rose Geranium Leaves.

Capture garden-fresh flavor and beauty in Rose Geranium Cake. The leaves accent the cake and frosting, and add a garnish.

Rose Geranium Frosting

1½ cups sugar
3 or 4 fresh rose geranium leaves
2 egg whites
⅓ cup cold water
¼ teaspoon cream of tartar
Dash salt
5 drops red food coloring

Pour *half* the sugar into a container with a tight-fitting cover. Wash leaves; add to sugar container. Cover with second half of sugar. Cover container. Let stand overnight. Remove rose geranium leaves before using sugar.

Place rose geranium sugar, egg whites, water, cream of tartar, and salt in top of double boiler (not over heat). Beat 1 minute with electric or rotary beater. Place over, but not touching boiling water. Cook, beating constantly, till frosting forms stiff peaks, about 7 minutes (do not overcook). Remove from boiling water. Add food coloring; beat till of spreading consistency. Frost cake.

Frosted Rose Geranium Leaves

Wash fresh rose geranium leaves; *thoroughly* pat dry. Carefully brush with 1 slightly beaten egg white; sprinkle with granulated sugar till well coated. Allow to dry and harden on wire rack. Store in airtight container.

ROSE HIP—The ripened fruit of a rose. Rose hip is the round, red part on the bush after the petals have fallen from the blossom. The cleaned and seeded rose hips are sold dried whole, cut, and powdered. They are used primarily in making jams and jellies.

ROSEMARY—An herb of the mint family. Rosemary has a warm, mintlike flavor and a spicy bouquet. The leaves resemble curved pine needles. They are about one inch long and are dark green in color.

Rosemary has been used in many ways since at least 500 B.C. It has been esteemed as a perfume, decoration, symbol of remembrance, and as a seasoning.

Legend says rosemary grows only in the gardens of the righteous. If you do not want to test the legend, you can purchase dried rosemary leaves at the supermarket. Use rosemary sparingly so it does not overwhelm the flavor of the food. Crushing the leaves and simmering or soaking them in a dish for at least 15 minutes helps to develop the full flavor.

Use rosemary with lamb, chicken, soups, stews, marinades, potatoes, cauliflower, turnips, peas, citrus fruits, spinach, and squash. (See also *Herb*.)

Turkey Timbales

2 beaten eggs
1 cup milk
½ cup quick-cooking rolled oats
1 cup chopped celery
1 tablespoon finely chopped onion
½ teaspoon salt
¼ teaspoon dried rosemary leaves, crushed
Dash pepper
2 cups ground cooked turkey
1 10½-ounce can condensed cream of mushroom soup
⅓ cup milk

Combine first 8 ingredients; add turkey and mix well. Pour into 4 greased 6-ounce custard cups. Bake at 350° for 45 to 50 minutes. Run spatula around timbales. Let stand 5 minutes before removing from cups. Combine mushroom soup and ⅓ cup milk in saucepan. Heat. Serve with timbales. Makes 4 servings.

Rosemary, an evergreen of the mint family, is native to the Mediterranean area. It grows as a tree or bush in warm climates.

Broiled Salmon Epicurean

 2 pounds fresh or frozen salmon
   steaks
 ¼ cup salad oil
 2 tablespoons lemon juice
 ½ teaspoon dried rosemary
   leaves, crushed
   Salt and pepper

Thaw frozen fish. Combine next 3 ingredients; shake well. Let stand at room temperature 1 hour; strain. Cut fish into 6 portions. Dip into oil mixture; sprinkle with salt and pepper. Place in a greased wire broiler basket. Grill over *medium-hot* coals about 5 to 8 minutes. Baste and turn. Brush other side; broil till fish flakes easily when tested with a fork, about 5 to 8 minutes longer. Makes 6 servings.

ROSETTE—1. Food formed into a shape similar to a rose. **2.** A thin pastry used as a dessert or as a shell for a main dish.

Tomatoes and radishes are good examples of foods formed into rosettes. By cutting through the skin four or five times, petals are formed. These make attractive relishes and garnishes for plates.

Pastry rosettes also are attractively shaped. They are made into elaborate designs by the mold on the rosette iron. These irons are heated, dipped into the thin batter, and placed into deep, hot fat for a short time. The crisp rosette is formed in the design of the iron.

Pastry rosettes become exotic desserts when sprinkled with confectioners' sugar, topped with a sauce, or served with fruit. They can also form the base for the main dish when used as a shell for a creamed meat mixture, such as chicken à la king.

Rosettes

 2 eggs
 1 tablespoon granulated sugar
 ¼ teaspoon salt
 1 cup sifted all-purpose flour
 1 cup milk
 1 teaspoon vanilla
   • • •
   Confectioners' sugar

Combine eggs, granulated sugar, and salt; beat well. Add flour, milk, and vanilla; beat smooth. Heat rosette iron in deep, hot fat (375°) for 2 minutes. Remove; drain off excess fat.

Then, dip hot iron into batter to ¼ inch from top of iron. Dip at once into hot fat (375°). Fry the rosette till golden, about ½ minute. Lift the iron out; tip it slightly to drain off any excess fat. With a fork push the rosette off the iron onto paper toweling placed on rack. Reheat iron for 1 minute; make next rosette. Sift confectioners' sugar over cooled rosettes. Makes 3½ dozen.

ROSETTE IRON—A long-handled metal utensil with a decorative disk screwed onto the handle. Most rosette irons come packaged with a wide variety of disks in elaborate designs, such as butterflies.

ROSE WATER—A liquid flavored and scented with roses. It is available at pharmacies and some specialty food stores.

You can use rose water to add a delightful, delicate flavor to cakes, pound cakes, jellies, custards, and confections. If you want to experiment with the flavor of rose water, substitute it in recipes calling for vanilla and almond extracts.

ROTARY BEATER—A kitchen utensil consisting of interlocking blades that are turned by a geared handle. Rotary beaters are used to whip eggs and other foods.

Mold crisp Rosettes into a variety of shapes simply by changing the disks that screw onto the end of the rosette iron.

ROTE—A pasta shaped like a wheel. Rote has a disk in the center with spokes running to the outside rim. (See also *Pasta*.)

ROTISSERIE *(rō tis' uh rē)*—An appliance with a motor-driven spit that is used for broiling foods. The spit rotates the food over, under, or in front of the heat, thus, ensuring even cooking and self-basting.

Rotisseries come in several forms. Some are portable appliances, which double as ovens and broilers. Other rotisseries are a special attachment on a barbecue grill or in the oven of a range. Depending on the appliance, the heat may be an electric heating unit, gas flame, or hot coals.

Rotisserie cooking is a dry-heat method that produces food with a delicious, crisp, brown exterior and a tender, moist interior. This method is suitable for tender cuts of meat, poultry, fruits, and vegetables. Some of the foods adapted to the rotisserie are chicken, duck, turkey, rolled roast, kabob assortments, crookneck squash, eggplant, pineapple, cherry tomatoes, and button mushrooms.

Mounting poultry correctly on the spit

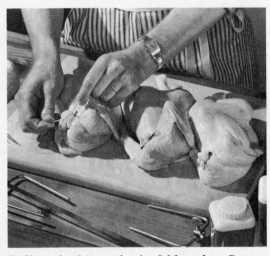

Pull neck skin to back; fold under. Secure skin to bird with a nail or skewer. Tie with a cord to hold the nail in place.

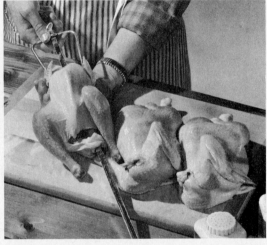

Place holding fork on rod, tines toward point; insert rod through bird (pinch tines together and push firmly into breast meat).

Using 24 inches of cord, start cord at back and loop around each wing. Make slipknots to secure wings. Tie in center; leave ends.

Using 18 inches of cord, loop around tail and then around crossed legs. Tie tightly to hold bird securely onto rod; leave ends.

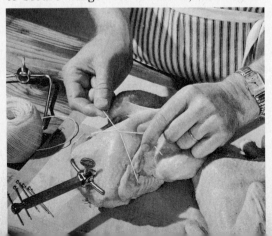

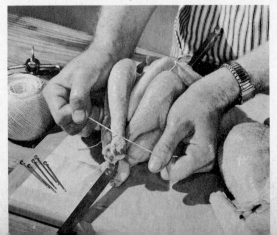

The instructions that come with your rotisserie will give explicit directions for operating the appliance. One of the important points is to be sure that the food is balanced on the spit. If it is not balanced, the food will flop on the spit and some parts, such as wings and legs of chickens, may char. Test the balance according to manufacturer's directions in the beginning and adjust the food until the spit turns smoothly.

When time is important, use your rotisserie to cook meals for the family and company. Foods cooked this way generally take less time than when they are roasted, so it helps to speed up meal preparation. It also gives a distinctive broiled or barbecued flavor to the food, which is as popular today as it was when the cavemen hung pieces of meat over a campfire.

Today, however, rotisserie cooking is surrounded with more glamour than in the past. People enjoy the special treat of watching while the food slowly turns and browns. You might take advantage of this by arranging for a party to be in the area of the rotisserie so that aroma and sight of the food cooking will whet the appetite of the guests. (See *Appliance*, *Barbecue* for additional information.)

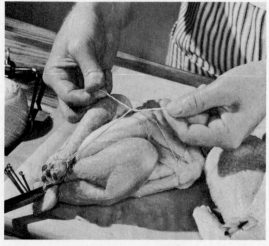

Pull together cords attached to wings and legs; tie tightly. Truss the bird neatly to avoid flying drumsticks or wings.

If cooking more than one bird, fasten others on spit in same way, using holding fork for each. Tighten thumbscrews with pliers.

Brush the birds well with salad oil for even browning and to hold the seasonings. Sprinkle well with salt, pepper, and paprika.

Brush the birds with a glaze or sauce several times during the last 30 minutes of cooking time on the rotisserie, if desired.

Spinning Chicken

Glaze chicken with a tangy basting sauce—

1 3- to 4-pound ready-to-cook
   whole broiler-fryer chicken
1 teaspoon salt
   Dash pepper
    •   •   •
½ cup chopped celery leaves
¼ cup snipped parsley
¼ cup chopped onion
2 tablespoons butter or
   margarine, melted
    •   •   •
¼ cup catsup
¼ cup corn syrup
2 tablespoons lemon juice
2 tablespoons salad oil
2 tablespoons prepared
   mustard

Rinse chicken and pat dry with paper toweling. Rub body cavity with salt and pepper. Combine celery leaves, parsley, onion, and melted butter; place in body cavity. Fasten neck skin to back with nail or skewer. Tie with cord to hold nail. To mount the chicken on the spit, place holding fork on rod, tines toward point; insert rod through the chicken (press tines firmly into the breast meat).

To tie wings, use 24 inches of cord. Start cord at back; loop around each wing tip. Make slipknots so wings can't straighten. Tie in center, leaving equal ends. Now, take an 18-inch piece of cord. Loop around tail, then around crossed legs. Tie very tightly to hold bird securely onto rod, leaving cord ends. Pull together cords attached to wings and legs; tie tightly. (If barbecuing more than one bird, fasten others on spit in same way, using holding fork for each; place birds close together.) Adjust holding forks and fasten screws tightly.

Test balance. Place chicken on the rotisserie, having *medium* coals at back and front of chicken and a drip pan under the revolving bird. Roast the chicken for about 2 hours without the barbecue hood or about 1¾ hours with the barbecue hood down.

Combine catsup, corn syrup, lemon juice, salad oil, and prepared mustard to make the basting sauce. Use the sauce to baste the chicken occasionally during the last 30 minutes of cooking. Makes 3 or 4 servings.

Spinning Ham

Begin the barbecue season early in the spring with fruit-flavored ham—

1 boneless, fully cooked ham
   or canned ham
    •   •   •
1 8¾-ounce can crushed
   pineapple
1 cup brown sugar
2 tablespoons prepared mustard
2 tablespoons lemon juice

Score ham, if desired. Tie ham at intervals with cord. Center ham lengthwise on rotisserie spit; fasten with holding forks. Adjust for balance. Let ham rotate over coals till heated through, allowing 10 minutes per pound.

Drain pineapple, reserving 2 tablespoons syrup. Mix crushed pineapple, reserved syrup, brown sugar, prepared mustard, and lemon juice. Brush pineapple glaze on ham occasionally during the last 20 minutes of cooking.

Grilled Rib Eye Roast

Herb butter complements an all-time favorite—

1 5- to 6-pound beef rib eye
   roast
½ cup butter or margarine,
   softened
2 teaspoons seasoned salt
1 teaspoon fines herbes
¼ teaspoon freshly ground
   pepper
   Few drops bottled hot pepper
   sauce

Tie rib eye roast with string at 1½-inch intervals. Center meat on spit; fasten with holding forks. Attach spit; turn on motor. Have *hot* coals at back of firebox and drip pan under roast. Roast 2 to 2½ hours for medium-rare or to your liking. Meat thermometer will register 140° for rare, 160° for medium, and 170° for well-done. Let roast stand 15 minutes to firm up before carving.

Meanwhile, blend softened butter, seasoned salt, fines herbes, pepper, and bottled hot pepper sauce. Dab a little of the herb butter on each serving—it's potent.

ROULADE *(r$\overline{oo}$ läd')*—A slice of meat spread with a filling, rolled up, and cooked. Roulade is made with various ingredients. Slices of beef, veal, pork, or fish are wrapped around a minced mixture such as ham, sausage, or cheese. The rolls are browned and simmered in wine or broth.

ROUND—The portion of the hind leg of a beef animal below the rump and above the shank. The corresponding section of pork, lamb, and veal is called the leg.

The round is cut into steaks and roasts or pot roast, or it is ground. These cuts may be divided into the top round (the inside portion) and the bottom round (the outside portion), which usually includes the eye of the round. The top round, within the same cut, is more tender than the bottom round. Most cuts from the round are best when braised. (See also *Beef.*)

ROUX *(r$\overline{oo}$)*—A blend of flour and fat that is cooked and used for thickening in sauces and gravies. Roux is used extensively in French and Creole cookery as the base for a variety of sauces. In mixing roux, butter, margarine, salad oil, or meat drippings and flour are mixed in equal parts. While the roux is cooking, stir it constantly so that it does not scorch, as this causes an unpleasant flavor and decreases the thickening power of the roux.

Roux can be cooked to three different shades, depending on its use. If the mixture is cooked for only a few minutes, it remains light. This type of roux is used in making light-colored sauces such as velouté. Heating the roux a few minutes longer gives it a light golden color. This blond roux is used in lightly colored sauces. Still longer cooking makes a rich, nut-colored sauce. The brown roux is used in making brown sauces. (See also *Sauce.*)

Steak Marchand De Vin

2 teaspoons butter or margarine
2 teaspoons all-purpose flour
1 cup beef broth *or* consommé

• • •

1 tablespoon chopped mushrooms
3 tablespoons Burgundy

⅓ cup cognac
1 teaspoon finely chopped shallots
½ bay leaf
Dash dried thyme leaves, crushed
2 peppercorns
1½ pounds sirloin steak, cut 1 inch thick

In a saucepan melt butter and blend in flour. Cook and stir over low heat till mixture browns. Add beef broth and bring mixture to boiling; cook 3 minutes, stirring constantly. Lower heat and simmer for about 20 minutes.

In another saucepan combine mushrooms and Burgundy; simmer the mixture till the liquid is reduced to half, about 5 minutes. Stir in brown sauce and remove from heat.

In a third saucepan combine cognac, shallots, bay leaf, thyme, and peppercorns. Cook till all liquid evaporates. Remove bay leaf and peppercorns. Add mushroom mixture; stir. Place steak in heavy skillet; cook 6 minutes on each side. Add 2 tablespoons cognac, if desired; set aflame. Pour sauce over. Serves 2.

RUE *(r$\overline{oo}$)*—A bitter herb. Rue has grayish green leaves, yellow flowers, a strong odor, and acrid flavor. Because of the strong, bitter flavor, use the leaves sparingly in chicken dishes, stews, salads, and cottage cheese. (See also *Herb.*)

RUM—An alcoholic liquor distilled from fermented sugar cane products. Rum ranges in color from a clear white to amber to mahogany. It varies from light to heavy in body and has a molasses flavor.

Rum was first made over 300 years ago in the West Indies. It soon became an important article of trade between the American colonies, West Indies, and Africa. Not all of the rum was traded to other countries, however. The colonists kept a lot for their own consumption—about four gallons per person each year.

Due to its widespread popularity, rum played a part in early American history. Because so much illicit rum was brought into the colonies, the British levied a tax on all rum imports. This tax was a major cause of the American Revolution.

How rum is produced: Rum is made from sugarcane—its juice, syrup, or molasses. The process is similar to the distilling of other liquors, except that rum does not need to be malted (changed from starch to sugar) since it is already a sugar. The sugarcane is fermented from 12 to 36 hours for light-bodied rums and up to 12 days for heavy-bodied rums. The liquor is then aged for one to four years in charred oak barrels. Caramel is added for color, but its flavor is so similar to molasses that it does not distort the taste. Then, the rum is aged in vats until ready for bottling. Most rum is bottled with the alcoholic content at about 80 proof.

Types of rum: Basically, there are three different types of rum. The first type is heavy, full-bodied, and dark. Jamaican rum, an example of this type, has a rich, full-molasses flavor. The second type is light-bodied and pungent. An example of this type, Bataria Arak, is made in the East Indies. The third type of rum is light, dry, and brandylike. There is a faint molasses taste. This rum is made in Puerto Rico and the Virgin Islands and accounts for about 70 percent of the rum sold in the United States.

The name on a rum bottle tells you its place of origin rather than its type. Cuban, Demerara, Martinique, and Haitian are

Please the most sophisticated tastes with a combination of rum and chocolate. Marble-Top Chocolate-Rum Pie will please the cook, too, since it is made ahead and refrigerated till later.

each from that respective area. Generally, certain types of rum are identified with certain areas—Cuban rums are light, while Jamaican rums are heavy. However, rums in *each area* are different primarily because of the variation in climate, water, and method of making liquor. Cubans also make a heavy rum.

Uses of rum: Rum is primarily used as a beverage. White liquor is often drunk straight in rum-producing countries, while people in the United States usually like it mixed with a fruit juice for use in punches and cocktails. Some of the more popular rum drinks are planters' punch, rum swizzle, daiquiri, bacardi, and the cold weather favorite, hot buttered rum.

Hot Buttered Rum

    1 piece stick cinnamon
    1 teaspoon sugar
    1 slice lemon peel
    2 jiggers rum (3 ounces)
      Boiling water
      Butter

In an old-fashioned glass combine cinnamon, sugar, lemon peel, and rum. Fill glass with boiling water; float butter pat atop. Serves 1.

The cooks of the world have also discovered uses for rum. It gives food a unique flavor when added to sauces, ice cream, candies, pies, and various desserts. The alcohol evaporates when the food is cooked, leaving only the molasses flavor. (See also *Wines and Spirits*.)

Rum-Eggnog Pie

In a bowl combine one 3¾- or 3⅝-ounce package *instant* vanilla pudding mix, 1¾ cups eggnog, and 1 tablespoon rum. Beat 1 minute. Pour into cooled, *baked* 9-inch pastry shell (see *Pastry*); chill till filling sets. Prepare one 2-ounce package dessert topping mix according to package directions. Beat in 1 teaspoon rum. Pile over pudding. Chill. Top with chopped candied fruit and toasted almonds.

Marble-Top Chocolate-Rum Pie

    ½ cup sugar
    1 envelope unflavored
        gelatin (1 tablespoon)
      Dash salt
    1 cup milk
    2 beaten egg yolks
    1 6-ounce package semisweet
        chocolate pieces (1 cup)
    ⅓ cup rum
    2 egg whites
    ¼ cup sugar
    1 cup whipping cream
    1 teaspoon vanilla
    1 *baked* 9-inch pastry shell,
        cooked (See *Pastry*)

In heavy saucepan combine the ½ cup sugar, gelatin, and salt. Stir in milk and egg yolks. Cook and stir over low heat till slightly thickened. Remove from heat. Add chocolate pieces; stir till melted. Add rum. Chill the mixture till it is partially set.

Beat egg whites till soft peaks form. Gradually add the ¼ cup sugar, beating till stiff peaks form. Fold into partially set chocolate mixture. Whip cream with vanilla. Layer whipped cream and chocolate mixture in pastry shell, ending with the whipped cream. Swirl the top to marble. Chill till firm. Garnish with additional whipped cream and semisweet chocolate pieces, if desired.

Peaches à la Rum

    3 tablespoons rum
    1 29-ounce can peach halves,
      drained
          • • •
    1 2-ounce package dessert
      topping mix
      Slivered, toasted almonds

Drizzle *2 tablespoons* rum over drained peach halves. Cover and chill for several hours. When ready to serve, prepare topping mix according to package directions. Stir in 1 tablespoon rum. Spoon some topping into 8 sherbet glasses. Top with peach half, rounded side down. Spoon additional topping in each peach cavity and sprinkle with slivered, toasted almonds. Serve cold. Makes 8 servings.

RUM FLAVORING—A commercially bottled liquid that has an imitation rum flavor. It is popular in desserts, frostings, and cakes. (See also *Flavoring*.)

RUMP—A cut of beef from the hindquarter. A rump roast is usually marketed as a rolled roast (bone removed, rolled, and tied) and seldom as a standing rump roast (bone in). This flavorful cut may be roasted if of top grade. However, if the roast is of a lower grade, braise it.

Plan on two servings from rump roast with bone and three servings from a roast without bone. (See also *Beef*.)

RUSK—A crisp, dry slice of bread. Rusks are made from a sweet or plain raised bread. The baked bread is sliced and baked again to dry it out and to brown it.

Rusks are available in packages in many supermarkets. Rusks are excellent bases for eggs Benedict and creamed meat, seafood, and poultry mixtures. Use rusk crumbs when making desserts.

RUSSET POTATO—An oblong potato with heavily netted skin, shallow eyes, and white flesh. Russet potatoes are so named because of their russet brown skin coloring. This potato category includes both the Norgold Russet and Russet Burbank species. The latter is known as the Idaho potato. (See also *Potato*.)

RUSSIAN COOKERY—Foods of Russia that are tinged with the grand cuisine of the days of the czars and with the individuality of the many geographical areas included in the vast nation, the United Soviet Socialist Republic. The national dishes range from elaborate desserts to simple soups and from the fare of a frozen land to that of a sub-tropical area.

Just how the Russian food pattern began to emerge is obscure. During the sixteenth century, Ivan the Terrible brought Italian workmen to Russia. They introduced Italian-styled pastries and frozen desserts, which became a favorite in Russia. German and French influences began to be felt late in the eighteenth century during the reign of Catherine the Great. The influence of Near East cookery is evident in the southern parts of Russia. Regardless of whether Polish foods were adopted by Russia or vice versa, there is a similarity between some of the dishes.

Out of these foreign influences, the conditions imposed by the weather, and the economics of the land, typical Russian foods have been developed.

Typical Russian appetizers: *Zakouska*, the Russian appetizer, consists of small portions of hot and cold foods. These are fork foods to be eaten while seated. An elaborate array, set out on a separate table at an occasion, might include a dozen varieties to be taken at will with small squares of thin white or dark bread.

An appetizer might include caviar, marinated herring, smoked sturgeon or eel, eggs with anchovies, shellfish in mayonnaise, patés, cucumbers or mushrooms in sour cream, vegetable salads, hot chicken livers, meatballs, and fish balls. Appetizers are usually accompanied by chilled vodka. At a simple home dinner, the array is not so lavish. Individual plates with an assortment of four appetizers are placed before each person.

Typical Russian soups: Soups are an important part of the Russian diet. At an elaborate Russian dinner, soup follows the zakouska. This course might include as many as three soups with a variety of both hot and cold soups.

For everyday meals, however, hearty soups are often the mainstay of the diet. Consequently, soups are frequently served as the main dish of the meal.

Vegetable soups are frequently found on the table. These are made with or without meat. Sometimes, a piece of meat that is cooked with the soup for flavor is removed and served at another meal. *Shchi*, cabbage soup, is made with fresh cabbage or sauerkraut as the base, and other vegetables are added if they are available.

Borsch, a classic soup of Russia, is always made with beets or with other vegetables accompanying the beets. *Smetana* (sour cream) is served with both shchi and borsch. *Rassolnik*, a tart meat soup, is flavored with pickles, olives, pickled mushrooms, and pickled cherries.

The Russians also prepare many cold soups. These usually are made with a base of *kvass*, a slightly fermented brew that is made from black or white bread.

Accompaniments for the soup are an important food in Russia, too. *Kasha* is one of the most commonly served accompaniments. In fact, it's considered one of the basic foods in the peasants' diets. Kasha is made by frying grain till browned and then baking it with a little water. A variety of grains are used. In the northern areas of Russia it is made of buckwheat groats. In some other areas, wheat or rice is used. But in the south it is made of corn.

Piroshki, a small, individual pastry pocket, is also served with soup. These are filled with minced meat, mushrooms, eggs, or cheese to blend with the flavor of the soup. Then, there are *pelmeri*, small dumplings, which are also filled and boiled in broth before being served.

Typical Russian meats: Russia has a variety of meats. The Ukraine and southern Russia provide pork, turkey, and smoked goose. The Caucasus have excellent lamb and mutton and some beef. Siberia has smoked bear. Throughout Russia, chickens, ducks, and furred and feathered game are available.

Russian meats are cooked many ways. Steaks are fried; beef filets, roasted. Cossack steaks are meat patties crumbed, fried, and served in a sour cream gravy with dill. Russian stew is made of crumbed and fried meat chunks, cooked with carrot, onion, and cubes of black bread.

The Russians often boil ham or bake it in a crust. Goose is stuffed with buckwheat groats. Instead of using apples in the filling, Russian cooks bake apples around the goose. Lamb is cooked in a pilaf, Turkish-style. Pork is cooked with sauerkraut with a piece of garlic-flavored sausage added. Game is roasted or braised. Some meats, especially lamb, are broiled on skewers.

Probably the two most famous Russian meat dishes are Beef Stroganoff, named for the Stroganov family of imperial Russia, and the excellent Chicken Kiev. The following recipe is a simplified version of the latter classic meat dish.

Chicken Kiev

4 large chicken breasts, boned, skinned, and halved lengthwise
2 tablespoons snipped parsley
¼ pound stick butter, chilled
 All-purpose flour
1 beaten egg
1 tablespoon water
½ cup fine dry bread crumbs

Place chicken breasts, boned side up, between two pieces of clear plastic wrap. Pound from center out to form cutlets not quite ¼ inch thick. Peel off wrap; season with salt.

Sprinkle parsley over cutlets. Cut cold butter into 8 sticks; place a stick at end of each cutlet. Roll meat as for jelly roll, tucking in sides. Press seam to seal well. Coat each roll with flour and dip in mixture of the egg and water. Then, roll in crumbs. Chill thoroughly, at least 1 hour. Fry chicken rolls in deep, hot fat (375°) till golden brown, about 5 minutes. Makes 4 to 8 servings.

Typical Russian fish: Fish and shellfish hold an important place in Russian cookery. Among the many species available throughout Russia are salmon, sturgeon, trout, pike, smelts, herring, and crayfish. These different varieties are enjoyed smoked and pickled as well as fresh.

One of the favorite fish products in Russia and also one of the most widely known is caviar. This roe from sturgeons and salmons is a delight that Russians savor on toast or crackers. It is included on the well-stacked zakouska table.

In Russian cookery, fish are often boiled and served either hot or cold. A horseradish cream or mustard sauce usually complements the fish. Other ways of cooking fish include poaching in wine, baking in pastry cases, frying, and steaming. Crabs are cooked in white wine, while crayfish are cooked in thyme-flavored sour cream and a wine sauce.

Kulebiaka is one of the classic fish dishes. Salmon is used for a filling inside the flaky pastry. For an authentic Russian meal, try serving sour cream with the recipe on the following page.

Kulebiaka

    2 tablespoons chopped onion
    3 tablespoons butter or
        margarine
 2¼ cups sifted all-purpose flour
    ¼ teaspoon dried dillweed
    1 cup milk
    2 tablespoons dry white wine
    1 16-ounce can red salmon,
        drained and flaked
    2 cups cooked rice
    1 3-ounce can sliced mushrooms,
        drained
    2 tablespoons snipped parsley
    ⅔ cup shortening
    1 beaten egg

In saucepan cook onion in butter till tender. Blend in ¼ *cup* flour, ½ teaspoon salt, and dillweed. Add milk. Cook and stir till thickened and bubbly; cook 1 minute more. Stir in wine, salmon, rice, mushrooms, and parsley. Sift together 2 cups flour and ½ teaspoon salt; cut in shortening till mixture resembles coarse crumbs. Gradually add ⅓ to ½ cup cold water, tossing with fork. Form into ball.

Roll dough between 2 pieces of waxed paper to a 20x10-inch rectangle. Remove top paper. Mound salmon mixture lengthwise down center third of rectangle. Fold one side of dough over salmon; peel paper back. Repeat with second side. Moisten edges with water; seal. Fold ends up; moisten and seal. Lifting paper, transfer to large greased baking sheet, seam side down. Peel off paper. Form into horseshoe shape; brush with egg. Prick top. Bake at 400° for 25 to 30 minutes. Serves 6 to 8.

Typical Russian breads: Breads are a basic food in Russia. The types and kinds are astoundingly numerous, with dark bread being the predominant variety. Added to this variety are whole grain and white breads baked in every shape.

One of the most popular types of bread is the Russian pancake, *blini.* These are not ordinary pancakes, but yeast-raised cakes made from buckwheat flour or a mixture of buckwheat and white flour. Blini are eaten with melted butter and fish, mushrooms with onions, or jam. Special occasions call for caviar filling.

Typical Russian desserts: Some of the most spectacular desserts appear during the Easter season. *Kulich* and *paskha* are the traditional Easter desserts.

Kulich is a special form of the tall Russian cake called a *baba.* The kulich, raised with yeast and rich with eggs, contains almonds, raisins, liqueur, and candied fruit peel. It is baked in a tall, round mold and comes out of the oven measuring about 12 inches. It is sometimes cut in horizontal slices to serve.

Paskha is served with the kulich. Paskha is made of cottage cheese, butter, sugar, eggs, cream, raisins, candied fruits, and almonds. The mixture is heated, then stirred to a velvety smoothness as it cools. It is then pressed into the traditional, wooden, pyramid-shaped mold, or into a gauze-lined flowerpot and left to drain off any excess liquid.

Other magnificent desserts include the charlotte and elaborate ice cream desserts. *Gureu Kasha,* a caramel-glazed farina pudding, is regarded by some to be the supreme Russian dessert.

Not all Russian desserts are as elaborate as these or as time consuming to make. Simplest and one of the most popular is the *kissel.* This pudding dessert is frequently served at family meals. It is made of puréed berries or other fruit and thickened with cornstarch. The berries commonly used are strawberries, apples, apricots, and rhubarb.

Vatruskhi, an individual pastry filled with cheese or fruit, is served with melted butter and sour cream. This is similar to American cheesecake. Fresh fruits in season are made into cooked compotes. Care is taken to keep the fruit pieces whole during cooking, and hot syrup is poured over uncooked fruit to preserve the shape. Sometimes, berries are served with sugar and wine for a simple dessert.

RUSSIAN DRESSING–A sharp-flavored salad dressing often containing chili sauce, peppers, chopped pimiento, chopped pickle, or caviar. Originally, this dressing was made with mayonnaise; however, today's dressing sometimes has a cooked base. Recipes for Russian dressing vary. (See also *Salad Dressing.*)

Russian Dressing

¼ cup sugar
3 tablespoons water
1½ teaspoons celery seed
½ teaspoon salt
½ teaspoon paprika
2½ tablespoons lemon juice
1 tablespoon Worcestershire sauce
1 tablespoon vinegar
1 cup salad oil
½ cup catsup
¼ cup grated onion

Cook sugar and water till mixture spins a thread (232°). Cool. Mix the remaining ingredients; beat in the sugar syrup. Chill thoroughly. Makes 2 cups salad dressing.

RUTABAGA—A root vegetable, relative of the turnip and member of the mustard family. Unlike turnips, rutabagas were developed fairly recently. It's believed they originated in Scandinavian regions during the seventeenth century. Some credence is given to this by the long-time use of the name Swede or Swede turnip for this vegetable. They are still grown widely in northern Europe, but in the Western Hemisphere production is limited to Canada and the United States.

Although rutabagas and turnips are used similarly, the yellow and white rutabaga varieties differ from turnips in size, shape, and color. They are larger and have a characteristic neck at the top. Yellow-fleshed rutabagas are usually bronze-skinned, but they can be green or purple; white-fleshed ones have a green skin.

Nutritionally, rutabagas are low in calories, only 35 to 1 cup cooked and cubed. They are a good source of vitamin C, while other vitamins and minerals are more sparingly represented.

When you buy rutabagas, look for roots that are heavy for size, firm and smooth, and free of cuts and blemishes. Select small or medium-sized ones in preference to large, overgrown rutabagas that tend to be woody and tough. Rutabagas are primarily a fall and late-winter crop and should be refrigerator-stored.

The flavor of rutabagas resembles that of turnip, except that it may be stronger. To prepare them for cooking, peel away the wax-coated skin down to the inner flesh of the root. To cook, peel and slice or cube. Add them to a saucepan with a small amount of boiling, salted water and cook, covered, for 25 to 40 minutes.

Try rutabagas and apples together for a blend of flavors with a slightly sweet taste. Or combine rutabagas and potatoes in a fluffy whip. (See *Turnip, Vegetable* for additional information.)

Rutabaga Whip

3 cups peeled, cubed rutabaga
3 cups peeled, cubed potato
2 tablespoons chopped onion
Light cream
Butter or margarine
Salt and pepper

Cook rutabaga, potatoes, and onion in boiling, salted water till tender, about 20 minutes. Drain and mash with cream and butter till light and fluffy. Season to taste with salt and pepper. Makes 4 to 6 servings.

Try a new vegetable dish to spruce up family meals. Rutabaga Whip combines potatoes and rutabaga for a tasty combination.

RYE—A cereal grain used for making flour and whiskey. Rye can be grown almost anywhere, but it is cultivated mainly in cold, damp climates. In the United States, rye is grown in North and South Dakota, Nebraska, Kansas, and Minnesota.

Rye flour: Rye is milled into flour for making breads, rolls, muffins, and crackers. The flour has a darker color than wheat flour. Bleaching during milling does not affect the color but does improve the baking qualities. Rye flour produces bread that has less volume and a more compact texture than wheat bread.

Light, medium, and dark rye flours are available on the market. These should be stored in the refrigerator or freezer. The maximum recommended storage time for rye flour is six months. When used, rye flour should be stirred with a spoon rather than sifted like wheat flour.

Pumpernickel is an example of a bread made entirely of rye flour. Most breads, however, are made with a combination of rye flour and another flour, such as wheat, for better volume and a milder flavor.

Light Rye Mixer Bread

      1 package active dry yeast
 1½ cups stirred rye flour
 2¼ cups sifted all-purpose flour
      1 tablespoon caraway seed
      1 teaspoon salt
 1¼ cups warm water
      2 tablespoons salad oil
      2 tablespoons honey

In large mixer bowl combine yeast, rye flour, ½ *cup* all-purpose flour, caraway, and salt. Mix together water, oil, and honey. Add to dry mixture in bowl. Beat ½ minute at low speed of electric mixer, scraping bowl constantly. Beat 3 minutes at high speed. Stir in the remaining all-purpose flour. Place the dough in greased bowl, turning once to grease surface. Cover; let dough rise till double, about 1 hour.

Punch down. Spread evenly in well-greased 9x5x3-inch loaf pan. Let rise till nearly double, about 30 to 35 minutes. Bake at 375° for 45 to 50 minutes. If bread browns too quickly, cover top loosely with foil.

Quick Swedish Rye Bread

      2 eggs
      1 13¾-ounce package hot roll mix
 ¾ cup medium rye flour
      1 tablespoon brown sugar
      2 tablespoons molasses
      1 to 2 teaspoons caraway seed

Using 2 eggs, prepare hot roll mix according to package directions. Stir in rye flour, brown sugar, molasses, and caraway seed. Let rise according to package directions. Turn out on floured surface, tossing lightly to cover dough with flour. Divide the dough in half; shape in loaves. Place the dough in two greased 8½x 4½x2⅝-inch baking dishes. Let rise according to package directions. Bake at 350° about 30 minutes. Makes 2 rye loaves.

Rye bread: Rye breads come in a variety of shapes and colors. They are molded into loaves, ovals with pointed ends, and rounds. The color varies from the almost-black pumpernickel to a light brown color.

Caraway seeds are a natural combination with rye breads. The seeds are usually included in commercial breads, and you can add them to suit your taste in homemade products. Another good flavor accent is orange. In Swedish cookery, a touch of orange peel is typical in rye bread.

The heavy texture, chewy crust, and distinctive flavor of rye bread makes it an appealing food. Appetizers made with rye bread are stimulating to the eye and the appetite. Rounds and triangles of rye or the party-sized bread are good for canapés and hors d'oeuvres, and with dips.

Toasty Rye Curls

      1 loaf tiny dark rye bread
 ½ cup butter or margarine,
        melted
      Dash garlic powder

With a very sharp knife, slice bread paper-thin. Place the bread in a single layer on baking sheet. Dry in a 300° oven till crisp, about 20 minutes. Combine butter and garlic powder; use mixture as a dip for rye slices.

Rye bread goes well with lunches and dinners, especially those including European foods. Try it spread with butter or margarine or even with sour cream in the European fashion. The flavor of rye bread is equally good as the base for a stuffing in the meat dish.

Ham with Rye Stuffing

   ¼ cup finely chopped onion
   3 tablespoons butter or margarine
   • • •
   1 beaten egg
   2 teaspoons prepared mustard
   ½ teaspoon caraway seed
   9 slices light rye bread,
      cubed (6 cups)
   1 fully cooked ham slice, cut 1½
      inches thick (2¼ pounds)

In a small saucepan cook onion in butter or margarine till tender but not brown. In a large bowl combine egg, mustard, caraway seed, and onion mixture. Add bread cubes; toss till thoroughly mixed. Shape the mixture into balls, using about ½ cup bread mixture for each ball. Place ham slice on rack in a shallow roasting pan. Bake at 325° for 20 minutes. Then, place the stuffing balls on rack around ham and bake 20 minutes more. Makes 6 servings.

Another popular use for rye bread is in sandwiches. The distinctive flavor of rye bread goes well with ham and cheese, braunschweiger, cold cuts, and other full-flavored fillings. Rye bread spread with cream cheese and topped with slices of smoked salmon makes an elegant lunch.

Nutritionally, rye bread contributes carbohydrates, minerals, and the B vitamins thiamine and riboflavin. There are 56 calories in a slice of rye bread and 40 calories in a slice of party rye measuring about 3 x 2 x ½ inches.

Rye whiskey: Rye is used in making rye whiskey and sometimes in making vodka. Rye whiskey must be made with at least 51 percent rye mash and be not more than 160° proof according to government regulations. Most of this liquor is made in the states of Pennsylvania and Maryland.

Rye whiskey comes in a variety of forms. Straight rye is heavier than bourbon, and it is not mixed with any other rye or liquor. Blended straight rye contains a combination of straight rye whiskeys. Blended rye contains other whiskeys and is lighter than straight rye.

In drinks, rye whiskey is used in making highballs, Manhattans, old-fashioneds, and whiskey sours. (See *Grain, Whiskey* for additional information.)

Slice Light Rye Mixer Bread into thin pieces. This full-flavored rye accented with honey and caraway seeds makes great sandwiches.

S

SABAYON *(sa ba yôn')* — The French version of zabaglione, an Italian sauce. Sabayon is made of egg yolks, sugar, and wine. The sauce is served hot over desserts, such as fruitcake, and cold over fruits. It also serves as a custardlike dessert when eaten alone. (See also *Zabaglione*.)

SACCHARINE *(sak'uh rin, -rīn')* — A white, crystalline compound that is approximately 500 times sweeter than sugar. Saccharine is a synthetic compound discovered at Johns Hopkins University in 1879. Since that time, it has been used as a sugar substitute for low-calorie diets, and in products such as tobacco.

A little saccharine goes a long way. It comes in powder, tablet, and liquid forms, which dissolve and blend easily in liquids. However, saccharine cannot be substituted as easily in baked products. You should select a recipe designed for a sugar substitute if you want to cut down on sugar in baked foods.

SABLEFISH — A saltwater flatfish found along the Pacific coast. Sablefish, often mislabeled Alaska black cod or butterfish, has a buttery texture and delicate flavor.

Sablefish, sold smoked and kippered, is used like smoked salmon in appetizers and sandwiches. Fresh fillets and steaks are best broiled, fried, or baked.

Nutritionally, sablefish contributes protein and the B vitamins thiamine and riboflavin. One 3½ ounce uncooked portion has 190 calories. (See also *Fish*.)

SACHER TORTE *(sä'kuhr tôr'tuh)* — A rich chocolate cake with an apricot filling, a chocolate frosting, and usually a garnish of whipped cream. This elegant dessert was created many years ago in Vienna, Austria, by a member of the Sacher family for whom the famous Sacher Hotel in that city was named. (See also *Torte*.)

Chocolate Torte Frosting

Frosting for the Sacher Torte—

  2 1-ounce squares unsweetened chocolate
  3 tablespoons butter or margarine
  3 cups sifted confectioners' sugar
     Dash salt
1½ teaspoons vanilla
  5 to 6 tablespoons boiling water

Melt chocolate and butter over hot water. Remove from heat. Stir in confectioners' sugar, salt, and vanilla. Gradually stir in enough boiling water to make thin frosting. (If frosting begins to thicken, add additional water.) Fill and frost Sacher Torte as directed.

Sacher Torte

        3 1-ounce squares unsweetened
            chocolate
        ⅔ cup sugar
        ½ cup milk
        1 beaten egg
                • • •
        ½ cup shortening
        1 cup sugar
        1 teaspoon vanilla
        2 eggs
                • • •
        2 cups sifted cake flour
        1 teaspoon baking soda
        ¼ teaspoon salt
        ⅔ cup milk
                • • •
        1 12-ounce jar apricot preserves,
            sieved
            Chocolate Torte Frosting
            Whipped cream

Combine unsweetened chocolate, the ⅔ cup sugar, ½ cup milk, and 1 beaten egg in a saucepan. Cook and stir over low heat till the chocolate melts and the mixture thickens; cool the mixture. Beat the ½ cup shortening to soften. Gradually add the 1 cup sugar, creaming till it is light and fluffy. Add the 1 teaspoon vanilla. Add the 2 eggs, one at a time, beating well after each addition.

Sift together flour, soda, and salt. Add to creamed mixture alternately with the ⅔ cup milk, beginning and ending with the flour mixture; beat well after each addition. Blend in chocolate mixture. Bake in 2 greased and floured 9x1½-inch round pans at 350° till done, about 25 to 30 minutes.

Cool layers thoroughly. Split each layer in two, using a thread (wrap around center of layer, crossing ends; pull).

Put cake together, spreading sieved apricot preserves, then about 2 tablespoons Chocolate Torte Frosting between each layer. Frost top and sides of cake with remaining frosting. Serve with generous dollops of whipped cream.

SACK *(sak)*—Sherry and other strong, light-colored, sweet wines. Sack (also sherris sack) was the name for sherry in sixteenth-century England. There are references to sack in Shakespeare's *Henry IV*.

Sack was introduced to England from Spain and the Canary Islands. It was one of the first sipping wines to become popular in that country. Today, the name sack is carried over as a brand name of a sherry. (See also *Sherry*.)

SADDLE—A large cut of meat including the two, undivided loins of an animal. Mutton, venison, lamb, and veal are the types of meat cut into saddles. Roasting is the usual method of cooking this tender cut.

SAFFLOWER—A thistlelike herb with orange red flowers. Safflower seeds are used in making a vegetable oil. Spanish and Polish people sometimes substitute safflower for saffron in their cooking.

SAFFLOWER OIL—A vegetable oil extracted from safflower seeds. It is polyunsaturated and is used in making margarine, shortening, and salad oil. One tablespoon of safflower oil has 124 calories. (See also *Fat*.)

SAFFRON *(saf' ruhn)*—The orange stigma of purple crocus flowers that is used as a spice. Saffron is considered the world's most expensive spice because these orange filaments must be carefully gathered by hand. There are only three filaments per flower and it takes at least 75,000 blossoms to make 1 lb. of saffron.

Saffron has been prized since ancient times. It was used in Babylon, Rome, and Greece for a dye in both cloth and food, for a perfume, and for a seasoning. The Moors introduced it to Spain and the Roman legions introduced saffron to England. Many classic dishes from these countries include saffron. Bouillabaisse from France and paella and arroz con pollo from Spain contain saffron.

American cooks use saffron to add a bright yellow color and a pleasantly bitter flavor to foods. The spice is used in flavoring breads, cakes, puddings, rice dishes, fish, and chicken.

The saffron available in American markets is imported from Spain and Portugal. It comes in two forms: tiny strands and powder. Packages of saffron mixed with rice are also available in supermarkets.

Pork Chops with Saffron Rice

6 pork chops, cut ½ to ¾ inch
　　thick
½ teaspoon salt
　Dash pepper
2 tablespoons shortening, melted
1 6-ounce package saffron rice
　　mix
½ cup chopped onion
　　• • •
1 beef bouillon cube
1¾ cups hot water
½ cup dairy sour cream

Sprinkle chops with salt and pepper. In skillet slowly brown chops in melted shortening; drain off excess fat. Add rice mix and onion. Dissolve bouillon cube in hot water; pour over rice. Bring to boiling; reduce heat.

Cover and cook over low heat for 40 minutes, stirring occasionally, till chops are tender and water is absorbed. Remove chops to warm platter; stir sour cream into rice mixture. Cook over low heat till heated. Makes 6 servings.

Always use the amount of saffron specified—a little bit adds a lot of flavor and too much causes a bitter, medicinal taste. If the saffron threads are not cooked in boiling liquid during preparation of a dish, heat some of the liquid and add the saffron. Let it stand about five minutes to dissolve before returning the liquid to the dish, as illustrated in the following recipes. (See also *Spice*.)

Saffron Bread

1 package active dry yeast
2½ to 3 cups sifted all-purpose
　　flour
1 cup milk
¼ cup sugar
2 tablespoons butter or margarine
½ teaspoon salt
⅛ teaspoon powdered saffron
　　• • •
¼ cup raisins
¼ cup currants
2 tablespoons chopped,
　　toasted almonds

In large mixer bowl combine yeast and 1½ *cups* flour. Heat milk, sugar, butter, salt, and saffron just till warm, stirring occasionally to melt the butter. Add to dry mixture in mixing bowl. Beat at low speed with electric mixer for ½ minute, scraping sides of bowl often.

Beat 3 minutes at high speed. By hand, stir in raisins, currants, almonds, and enough of the remaining flour to make a soft dough. Knead till smooth and elastic, 8 to 10 minutes. Place in greased bowl; turn once to grease surface. Cover and let rise in warm place till double, about 1¾ hours. Punch down; turn out on lightly floured surface. Cover and let rest 10 minutes. Shape in loaf; place in greased 8½x 4½x2½-inch loaf dish. Let rise till double, about 1¼ hours. Bake at 375° till done, about 35 minutes. If necessary to prevent over-browning, cover with foil for last 15 minutes.

SAGE—An herb belonging to the mint family. The slender, grayish green leaves of sage give foods in which it is used a pungent, slightly bitter flavor.

Sage has been credited with many virtues through the centuries. It was once used as a medicine to lengthen one's life and also to improve the memory. This is noticeable in the traditional Christmas and Thanksgiving Day meat stuffings.

Sage has slender green leaves that turn a grayish color when dried. The plant has blue flowers and grows to a height of two feet.

Sage's value as a seasoning has made it one of the most popular herbs in America. It goes well with pork and stuffings.

Sausage Stuffing

  ½ **pound bulk pork sausage**
 18 **cups soft bread crumbs**
  2 **cups diced apples**
  1 **cup chopped onion**
  ½ **cup raisins**
    Giblets, cooked, drained (reserve
      ½ cup broth), and chopped
  4 **teaspoons salt**
  2 **teaspoons ground sage**
  ¼ **teaspoon pepper**
  3 **beaten eggs**

Cook sausage until it is lightly browned; drain. Add crumbs, apples, onion, raisins, giblets, and seasonings. Add eggs and reserved giblet broth; toss the stuffing to moisten. Enough stuffing for one 20-pound turkey.

Sage also accents poultry, cheese, meat loaves, breads, and vegetables such as brussels sprouts, carrots, and tomatoes. When adding sage, do not use too much or its flavor will dominate the food's flavor.

Several forms of sage, most of which are from Yugoslavia and southern Europe, are available in supermarkets. There are dried sage leaves, rubbed sage, and ground sage. The rubbed form is fluffy, while ground is finer in texture. You can grow sage plants in a home garden easily. (See also *Herb.*)

Herb Twists

  1 **13¾-ounce package hot roll mix**
  1 **teaspoon rubbed sage**
  ½ **teaspoon dried basil leaves,**
    crushed
  2 **tablespoons butter or margarine,**
    melted

Prepare hot roll mix according to package directions, *adding* sage and basil to the dry mix. Turn out on lightly floured surface; knead till smooth, about 2 to 3 minutes.

Place dough in greased bowl, turning once to grease surface. Cover and let rise in warm place till double, about 45 minutes. Punch down. Cover; let rest 10 minutes. Turn out on lightly floured board. Roll to 18x8-inch rectangle. Brush *half* the dough, lengthwise, with melted butter. Gently fold unbuttered half over buttered to make 18x4-inch rectangle.

Slice dough crosswise into 1-inch wide strips. Holding strips by ends, twist several times; place on greased baking sheet. Let rise in warm place for 20 minutes. Bake at 425° till golden brown, about 8 to 10 minutes. Cool slightly on rack before serving. Makes 18 rolls.

SAGE CHEESE—A young Cheddar cheese flavored with sage. Sage cheese has a sharp flavor that connoisseurs appreciate.

This cheese is also called Vermont sage and, sometimes, green cheese because the cheese is mottled green. This coloring once was due to the leaves of sage. Now, a sage extract flavors the cheese and green corn or alfalfa contributes color.

SAGO *(sā' gō)*—A dried, starchy substance made from the soft center of palms, and grown in the East Indies and Indonesia.

Sago is the basic food in the southwest Pacific. The people use it in making soups and cakes. In North America, sago is used occasionally in thickening puddings.

SAINT JOHN'S BREAD—A long fruit pod grown on a tree native to the Mediterranean. This fruit is also called carobs.

The dried pods consisting of hard seeds and a sweet pulp are eaten like raisins or are ground into flour.

SAKE *(sä'kē)*—A Japanese alcoholic beverage that is brewed from rice. Sake, the national beverage of Japan, is also called rice wine. However, it more closely resembles beer than wine.

Sake is colorless with a slightly sweet flavor and a faintly bitter aftertaste. It contains from 12 to 16 percent alcohol.

Custom is to serve sake before a meal in small porcelain cups. The drink is usually warmed to about 100°. Sake is popular as a flavoring in sauces and cocktails. (See also *Wines and Spirits.*)

SALAD

A wide variety of salad appetizers, side dishes, main dishes, and desserts.

A salad can be as simple as a bowl of greens dressed with oil and vinegar or lettuce or spinach leaves sprinkled with salt and eaten with the fingers, or as elaborate as a beautiful arrangement of vegetables, poultry, or seafood, a fancy gelatin mold, or a frozen delight. Although the traditional definition of a salad is a dish put together with a complementary dressing, today, the category salad also includes dishes that are not served with a dressing. In fact, there are an endless variety of salads, ranging from hot to frozen and from meat to fruit, which use an equally endless array of ingredients.

Salads of one kind or another have been enjoyed for centuries. Ancient Greeks and Romans ate salads made of greens. The Greeks, who regarded salad as food for the gods, often served it as the final course to clear the palate after sweets. A book of recipes written by a Roman during the first century mentions that salads, like many other foods at that time, were considered to have medicinal value. The Romans are also responsible for the name salad. Because these people sprinkled salt on greens as a salad dressing, the Latin word for salt, *sal*, was eventually expanded to salad as a name for this dish.

Although salads appeared during the ancient times, few salads were served during the Middle Ages. Even during the revival of interest in food that occurred in the Renaissance, it took quite awhile before salads were a fairly common menu item. By the late-seventeenth century, salads had become so popular that a book, *Acetaria, a Discourse on Sallets*, was written about them.

During the eighteenth century, salads gained popularity in Europe. This was a time of experimentation, and several different ingredients, seasonings, and dressings for salads were introduced. French and other European chefs sometimes concocted salads that had well over two dozen ingredients.

Salad-making remained primarily a European art until the late 1800s when wealthy Americans began importing French salad chefs. However, it still took several decades for salads to become a common menu item in America. Today, the people of the United States probably eat more salads than any other group of people. The traditional tossed salads, coleslaw, gelatin salads filled with fruits and vegetables, bean salads, pea salads, macaroni salads, potato salads, meat salads, seafood salads, egg salads, and numerous fruit combination salads are only a few of the salads that are enjoyed in this country today.

Salads are also a popular part of the menu in other countries. For example, Canadians relish sweet-savory salads such as tomatoes and oranges with a dressing of tomato sauce and orange juice. In France, the traditional salad of greens served with an oil and vinegar dressing remains the favorite. The Spanish enjoy vegetable combination salads such as tomatoes with beans. As can be seen from these examples, a compilation of the thousands of salad recipes used around the world would indeed be a diverse collection.

Crisp tossed salad

← Serve delectable Tossed Western Salad as an appetizer or side dish. Marinated artichokes and croutons make this salad special.

Tossing tips

Add extra flavor to your salads with this trick. Sprinkle salt into a wooden salad bowl. Then, using the back of a spoon, mash a garlic clove into the salt. As the salad is tossed, it acquires a garlic flavor.

Place salad ingredients in a big bowl, add dressing, then mix using a roll-toss. To get the required down-and-over motion, use two salad tools and stroke down with one as the other comes up and over.

Enhance the appearance of tossed salads by tearing the salad greens into bite-sized pieces rather than by cutting them with a knife. Torn greens make a fresh-tasting salad that absorbs the dressing easily.

If the salad includes tomatoes, avoid diluting the dressing by reserving the juicy wedges or slices for a garnish. Give the salad crunch by adding crisp croutons or chopped walnuts lightly browned in butter.

Before adding oil-based dressings to the salad, shake them to emulsify the oil and vinegar and blend the other ingredients. Pour just enough dressing over the salad to lightly coat the greens; then toss gently.

If tossing the salad has to wait awhile, keep the torn salad greens fresh by covering them with damp paper toweling wrung out in ice water. For delays that are very long, refrigerate the bowl of covered greens.

Preparation

As was pointed out previously, salads are made from a wide variety of ingredients. Even so, they can be divided into five types – vegetable combinations; fruit combinations; meat, poultry, fish, and egg salads; gelatin salads; and frozen salads.

Vegetable combinations: In the United States, the most popular kind of salad is a crisp salad made of greens and other raw vegetables, and tossed with a salad dressing. By far the most common ingredient in tossed salad is iceberg lettuce. However, if you want to give variety to the salad, use a mixture of greens including Bibb lettuce, red lettuce, romaine, curly endive, escarole, watercress, or spinach. In addition to fresh greens, use other ingredients such as shredded carrot and red cabbage, sliced radish, sliced cucumber, crisp croutons, green pepper rings, ripe olives, crumbled bacon, and shredded cheese to add colors and flavors.

One of the most important parts of a tossed salad is the dressing. Even though choosing from the numerous types of salad dressings may be difficult, remember to choose a dressing that complements but does not overpower the other ingredients. (See also *Salad Dressing.*)

Preparing a fresh, crisp tossed salad is simple if you use the following tips. Several hours before the meal, carefully wash the salad greens in cool water, and then dry them by shaking them in a wire salad basket or by gently patting them with a kitchen towel. Next, store the greens in the refrigerator to crisp them. (Wilted greens don't have the appealing appearance that crisp greens do, so be sure to allow several hours of chilling.)

Shortly before serving time, tear the greens into bite-sized pieces. (Don't cut them with a knife as this hastens darkening of the edges.) Also, prepare the other vegetables for the salad. At serving time, gently toss the greens, other ingredients, and dressing together. Although you usually toss the salad in the kitchen, why not stage a small production by tossing the salad at the dinner table while your dinner guests watch?

Tossed Salad Combination Guide		
Venture into the realm of leafy greens and vegetables with a flavorful salad creation that will give each menu spark and variety. To prepare the winning combinations given below, tear salad greens in bite-sized pieces unless otherwise indicated. Add remaining ingredients *except* garnish and toss lightly with your favorite dressing. Garnish the salad with the ingredient that is recommended in the last column; serve the tossed salad immediately.		
To Go Along With	**Add These**	**Garnish With**
Bibb lettuce	Tomato, cut in wedges Unpared cucumber, sliced Avocado, peeled and sliced	Hard-cooked egg, sliced
Boston lettuce	Hard-cooked egg, chopped Fresh mushrooms, sliced Chives, snipped	Parsley sprigs
Boston lettuce	Watercress Anchovy fillets	Parmesan cheese, grated
Chinese cabbage	Leaf lettuce Celery, bias-cut Radishes, sliced Chives, snipped	Water chestnuts, sliced
Curly endive	Iceberg lettuce Bacon, crisp-cooked and crumbled Tomato, cut in wedges Celery, sliced Radishes, sliced Green onion, chopped	Hard-cooked egg, sliced
Iceberg lettuce	Carrot, shredded Celery, diced Mandarin oranges, well-drained	Raisins

Iceberg lettuce	Raw cauliflowerets,
	    thinly sliced
	Onion, sliced and separated
	    into rings
	Pimiento-stuffed green
	    olives, sliced
		Blue cheese, crumbled

Tossed Salad Combination Guide		
To Go Along With	Add These	Garnish With
Leaf lettuce	Chicory Watercress Tomato, cut in wedges Onion, thinly sliced Cucumber, sliced	Walnut halves
Leaf lettuce	Curly endive Tomato, finely diced Green onion, sliced	Cheddar cheese, cut in thin strips
Leaf lettuce	Watercress Raw spinach Carrot curls Pitted ripe olives, sliced	Almonds, toasted
Romaine	Tomato, diced Green pepper, chopped Romano cheese, grated	Artichoke hearts
Raw spinach	Bacon, crisp-cooked and crumbled Hard-cooked egg, chopped Carrot, thinly sliced	Canned French-fried onions
Raw spinach, shredded	Raw zucchini, sliced Radishes, sliced Green onion, sliced	Mushroom crowns
Raw spinach	Leaf lettuce Romaine Artichoke hearts Pimiento, chopped Celery, sliced	Pimiento-stuffed olives, sliced
Watercress	Iceberg lettuce Ripe olives, sliced Cucumber, sliced Tomatoes, cut in wedges Green pepper rings Green onion, sliced	Croutons

Tossed Western Salad

Cook one 9-ounce package frozen artichoke hearts according to package directions; drain. In screw-top jar combine ½ cup salad oil; ¼ cup lemon juice; 3 tablespoons tarragon vinegar; 2 tablespoons sugar; 2 tablespoons minced onion; 1 clove garlic, crushed; 1 teaspoon salt; ½ teaspoon dry mustard; and dash freshly ground pepper. Cover; shake. Pour over artichokes. Cover; chill well, stirring occasionally.

Several hours before serving, wash 3 heads Bibb or 2 heads Boston lettuce and 2 medium heads romaine. Drain well on paper toweling. Tear greens into bite-sized pieces and layer with paper toweling in large container. Cover with damp paper toweling; refrigerate. Slice ½ bunch radishes. Place in bowl; cover and chill. Slice 1 avocado and place in another small bowl. Sprinkle with a little of the artichoke dressing. Cover and chill. Brown 1 cup packaged croutons in 2 tablespoons butter, stirring till toasted on all sides.

To serve, fluff greens into bowl; add artichokes with dressing and radishes. Roll-toss. Season with salt and freshly ground pepper. Add avocado and croutons; toss. Serves 8.

Tossed green salads are by no means the only kind of vegetable salad. In fact, almost all vegetables are adaptable for use in salads. Everyone is familiar with the standard coleslaw, bean salad, and potato salad. However, perk up the standards by adding ingredients such as tomato, pineapple, or peanuts to coleslaw; pimiento or olives to bean salad; and cauliflower, cheese, or cucumber to potato salad.

Also try different combinations of other vegetables such as asparagus, corn, cauliflower, peas, tomatoes, radishes, cucumbers, celery, onion, green pepper, beet, carrot, and broccoli.

Italian Bean Toss

Cook two 9-ounce packages frozen Italian green beans according to package directions; drain and chill. Blend together ½ cup mayonnaise, 2 tablespoons grated Parmesan cheese, 1 tablespoon finely chopped canned pimiento, 1 teaspoon salt, and ¼ teaspoon curry powder. Add beans and toss; chill. Serves 6 to 8.

Potato Salad Special

Combine 3 cups diced cooked potatoes; 1½ cups sliced raw cauliflower; 1 cup diced celery; 2 hard-cooked eggs, chopped; ¼ cup chopped onion; and 6 slices bacon, crisp-cooked and crumbled. In small bowl mix 1 cup mayonnaise, 1 tablespoon bacon drippings, and 2 teaspoons caraway seed (optional); pour over salad. Toss lightly. Salt to taste. Chill. Serves 5 or 6.

Bean and Avocado Boats

Combine ¼ cup salad oil, 2 tablespoons vinegar, 2 tablespoons lemon juice, 1 tablespoon sugar, ½ teaspoon chili powder, ¼ teaspoon salt, dash garlic salt, and dash pepper. Pour over one 15-ounce can garbanzo beans, drained; one 8-ounce can kidney beans, drained; and 2 tablespoons sliced green onion. Chill well, stirring occasionally. Spoon beans into 2 avocados, halved lengthwise and seeded. Serves 4.

Fruit combinations: For a refreshing salad, select fruits from the wealth of fresh, canned, dried, and frozen fruits available and combine them with a tart-sweet dressing, dairy dressing, or cooked dressing. For a change from the salad-in-a-bowl, capitalize upon the appealing colors and shapes of various fruits by serving the salad in an attractive arrangement with a bowl of dressing.

Fresh fruits make particularly delicious salads. Although fruits such as bananas and some citrus fruits are widely available all year, many other fruits are seasonal. For example, watermelons, cantaloupes, peaches, strawberries, raspberries, and cherries are summer favorites, while apples, pears, cranberries, and pomegranates are more plentiful in the fall and winter. A salad that uses fresh fruits is a flavorful addition to any menu.

A make-ahead salad

As its name indicates, 24-Hour Salad should → be made a day before serving. Chilling the salad overnight allows the flavors to blend.

Fruit Combination Guide

Team the fruit with suggested counterparts at the right for a real taste treat. Then, arrange items on different varieties of greens each time. Top with a dressing.

To Go Along With	Choose These
Apple, diced	• Mandarin orange sections and diced celery
Unpeeled red apple slices	• Grapefruit sections, sliced avocado, and pomegranate seeds
Avocado, peeled and sliced	• Grapefruit sections and persimmon wedges • Sliced tomato
Apricots, halved and seeded	• Red grapes and sliced jellied cranberry sauce • Pineapple chunks and maraschino cherries
Banana, halved lengthwise	• Orange and grapefruit sections and pitted dates • Cottage cheese and salted peanuts
Banana, bias-cut	• Halved red plums, sliced pineapple, red raspberries, and coconut
Figs, halved and seeded	• Raspberries and cream cheese balls rolled in shredded coconut
Grapefruit sections	• Sweetened raw cranberries • Orange sections, pineapple spears, and ripe olives
Honeydew melon, peeled and crescent-cut	• Thinly sliced Prosciutto ham
Honeydew melon, peeled and sliced	• Raspberry, lemon, or lime sherbet
Melon, peeled and sliced	• Fresh sweet cherries, halved green grapes, and chopped pecans • Fruit cocktail and whipped cream
Melon, cubed	• Cottage cheese and fresh strawberries • Raspberries and bias-cut banana slices
Peach, halved	• Blueberries and raspberries • Cottage cheese and candied ginger
Peach, spiced	• Pineapple chunks and apple-mint jelly
Pear, halved	• Shredded American cheese • Sliced plums and blueberries • Halved green grapes and cream cheese
Pineapple, chunks	• Orange sections and fresh strawberries
Pineapple, sliced	• Watermelon chunks and sliced banana

24-Hour Salad

1 20½-ounce can pineapple tidbits
3 egg yolks
2 tablespoons sugar
2 tablespoons vinegar
1 tablespoon butter or margarine
    Dash salt
1 16-ounce can pitted light
    sweet cherries, drained
2 peeled oranges, cut up and
    drained
¼ cup drained maraschino cherries
2 cups miniature marshmallows
1 cup whipping cream

Drain pineapple tidbits, reserving 2 table-spoons syrup. In top of double boiler beat egg yolks slightly; add reserved syrup, sugar, vinegar, butter or margarine, and salt. Place over *hot, not boiling* water; cook, stirring constantly, till mixture thickens *slightly* and *barely* coats a metal spoon (about 12 minutes). Cool to room temperature.

Combine *well-drained* fruits and marshmallows. Pour cooled custard over and mix gently. Whip cream; fold into fruit. Turn into serving bowl. Cover and chill 24 hours. Trim with fresh strawberry halves and seedless green grapes, if desired. Makes 6 to 8 servings.

Yogurt–Fruit Combo

Easy dressing is made of yogurt and mayonnaise—

2 8-ounce cartons orange yogurt
⅓ cup mayonnaise or salad
    dressing
1 11-ounce can mandarin orange
    sections, drained
1 20-ounce can pineapple tidbits
    drained
1 16-ounce can pitted light
    sweet cherries, drained
    and halved
1 cup miniature marshmallows

Stir together orange yogurt and mayonnaise or salad dressing. Fold in mandarin oranges, pineapple tidbits, light sweet cherries, and miniature marshmallows. Chill at least one hour before serving. Makes 10 to 12 servings.

Date–Apple Waldorf

1 orange
2 cups diced, unpeeled apple
    (about 2 apples)
½ cup pitted dates, snipped
½ cup chopped celery
⅓ cup chopped walnuts
    • • •
¼ cup mayonnaise or salad
    dressing
1 tablespoon sugar
¾ cup frozen whipped dessert
    topping, thawed

Peel orange; section over bowl to catch juices. Halve orange sections and reserve 1 tablespoon juice. In medium bowl combine apple, dates, celery, walnuts, and orange sections. Blend together mayonnaise, sugar, and the reserved orange juice. Fold in the thawed whipped dessert topping; combine with date mixture. Serve in lettuce cups. Makes 6 servings.

Meat, fish, poultry, and egg salads: When the menu calls for a hearty salad, turn to recipes that contain meat, fish, poultry, or egg. With choices such as chicken, turkey, or egg salad dressed with mayonnaise, a shrimp salad with an herb-vinegar dressing, a salad of meat, cheese, greens, and other vegetables dressed with French dressing, and a ham and cheese combination, you are sure to find just the right salad.

Leftover meats, such as roast beef and poultry, are adaptable to salads, too. Simply combine them with other ingredients such as salad greens, tomatoes, pickles, cheese, onion, or green pepper; then add a compatible dressing. These salads are more attractive if you cut the ingredients in bite-sized pieces.

Ham and Egg Salad

Combine 1½ cups cubed fully cooked ham; 6 hard-cooked eggs, coarsely diced; ½ cup chopped celery; and ½ cup chopped sweet pickle. Blend together ⅓ cup mayonnaise or salad dressing and 2 tablespoons prepared mustard. Toss with ham mixture. Chill. Serves 4.

San Marino Beef Salad

    4 to 5 pounds beef short ribs
    1/3 cup chopped carrot
    1/3 cup chopped onion
         • • •
    1/4 cup olive oil
    1/4 cup red wine vinegar
    1/2 teaspoon dry mustard
    1/2 teaspoon salt
        Dash cayenne
    1 medium red onion
    1/2 sweet red pepper
    3 medium carrots
    3 branches celery
    2 tablespoons cut celery leaves

In large saucepan cover beef short ribs, chopped carrot, and chopped onion with salted water. Bring to a boil. Cover and simmer till meat is tender, about 1½ to 2 hours. Strip meat from bone and trim off fat. Cut meat into julienne strips (3 cups); chill.

In a screw-top jar combine the ¼ cup olive oil, wine vinegar, dry mustard, salt, and cayenne. Shake well; chill. Shake again before using. Slice red onion and separate into rings. Cut red pepper, carrots, and celery branches into julienne strips.

To serve combine beef strips, onion rings, and the pepper, carrots, and celery strips. Toss with dressing. Sprinkle with cut celery leaves. Makes 4 servings.

Turkey-Mushroom Salad

    2½ cups cubed cooked turkey
    1½ cups sliced fresh mushrooms
    1 cup chopped celery
    2 tablespoons sliced pimiento-
        stuffed green olives
    1/3 cup mayonnaise or salad
        dressing
    1 tablespoon lemon juice
    1 teaspoon finely chopped onion
    1/2 teaspoon salt
        Romaine leaves

Combine turkey, mushrooms, celery, and olives. Blend mayonnaise, lemon juice, onion, and salt. Add to turkey mixture; toss lightly. Chill. Line salad bowl with romaine. Spoon in turkey salad. Makes 6 servings.

Crab-Wild Rice Salad

    1 6-ounce package long-grain,
        wild rice mix
    1 7½-ounce can crab meat, drained,
        flaked, and cartilage removed
    1 tablespoon lemon juice
    1/4 cup chopped green pepper
    1/4 cup chopped canned pimiento
    2 tablespoons snipped parsley
    1/2 cup mayonnaise or salad
        dressing
    2 tablespoons Russian salad
        dressing
    1/2 teaspoon salt
    2 medium avocados, peeled and
        sliced*

Cook rice following package directions; cool. Mix together crab meat and lemon juice. Combine rice, crab, green pepper, pimiento, and parsley. Blend together mayonnaise, Russian salad dressing, and salt. Add mayonnaise mixture to vegetable-crab mixture and toss lightly. Chill. Serve with avocado slices. Serves 4 or 5.

*To keep avocado slices bright, dip in lemon juice mixed with a little water.

Gelatin salads: A mold of gelatin, with or without added ingredients, makes an enticing salad for any meal. When the meal is large, serve a simple salad of fruit-flavored gelatin. On the other hand, when the rest of the meal is light, serve a hearty salad of fruits, vegetables, meat, or cheese with a base of either unflavored or flavored gelatin.

Although gelatin is clear, ingredients such as whipped cream, ice cream, cream cheese, and mayonnaise give gelatin salads a creamy, opaque appearance as well as adding a delectable flavor to the gelatin. As a general rule, whipped cream and ice cream are particularly compatible with fruits, and mayonnaise is most commonly used with vegetables. However, whipped cream, ice cream, mayonnaise, and cream cheese can all be used with a wide variety of gelatin flavors and added ingredients.

Since gelatin requires several hours of refrigeration to set, this type of salad must be prepared quite awhile before it is served. However, if time is shorter than usual, you can hasten the setting of gelatin salads. Simply dissolve a 3-ounce package of flavored gelatin in 1 cup boiling water; then, add 8 to 12 ice cubes and stir constantly until the gelatin starts to thicken (this usually takes 2 to 3 minutes). Remove the unmelted ice and let stand at room temperature for about 5 minutes before folding in fruits and vegetables; then chill.

Harvest Fruit Mold

> 1 11-ounce package mixed dried fruits
> ⅓ cup sugar
> 2 3-ounce packages orange-flavored gelatin
> 2 cups boiling water

In saucepan combine fruit and enough water to cover; simmer gently, covered, 25 to 30 minutes, adding sugar for last 5 minutes of cooking. Drain fruit, reserving syrup. Add water to syrup to make 2 cups. Dissolve gelatin in the 2 cups boiling water; stir in syrup mixture. Chill till partially set.

Pit prunes; cut up all fruit. Fold fruit into gelatin. Pour into 6-cup ring mold; chill till firm. Makes 8 servings.

Confetti Relish Mold

> 1 3-ounce package lemon-flavored gelatin
> 2 beef bouillon cubes
> 1 cup boiling water
> 1 tablespoon tarragon vinegar
> 1 cup dairy sour cream
> ½ cup chopped, unpeeled cucumber
> ¼ cup sliced radishes
> ¼ cup finely chopped green pepper
> 2 tablespoons sliced green onion

Dissolve gelatin and bouillon cubes in boiling water; stir in vinegar. Chill till partially set. Add sour cream to gelatin; beat with rotary beater till smooth. Fold in chopped cucumber, sliced radishes, chopped green pepper, and sliced green onion. Pour into a 3½-cup mold. Chill till firm. Makes 6 servings.

Shrimp in Avocado Ring

Dissolve one 3-ounce package lemon-flavored gelatin in 1 cup boiling water. Chill till partially set; whip till fluffy. Stir in 1 cup mayonnaise or salad dressing, 1 to 2 tablespoons lemon juice, and ½ teaspoon salt.

Whip 1 cup whipping cream. Fold whipped cream and 2 medium avocados, peeled and sieved (1 cup), into gelatin mixture. Pour into one 5½-cup ring mold or six to eight ½-cup ring molds. Chill till firm. Unmold on lettuce-lined plate; fill center with cleaned, cooked shrimp. Makes 6 to 8 servings.

Potato Salad Mold

Pimiento-stuffed olives add color and flavor—

In saucepan mix 1 envelope unflavored gelatin (1 tablespoon), 2 tablespoons sugar, and ¾ teaspoon salt. Add 1¼ cups water; stir over low heat till gelatin and sugar are dissolved. Add ¼ cup lemon juice. Cool to room temperature. Stir 4 cups diced, peeled, cooked potatoes; ¾ cup chopped celery; 3 hard-cooked eggs, chopped; ¼ cup sliced pimiento-stuffed green olives; ¼ cup chopped green pepper; and ¼ cup snipped parsley into gelatin mixture.

Whip ½ cup whipping cream. Fold whipped cream and 1 cup mayonnaise into gelatin. Spoon mixture into a 7½-cup mold or 9x9x2-inch pan. Chill till firm. Makes 8 or 9 servings.

Frozen salads: When the menu demands something refreshingly cold, serve a frozen salad. The smooth iciness of this type of salad depends on the inclusion of ingredients (interfering agents) that prevent the formation of large ice crystals. One of the ingredients most commonly used is whipped cream. A pudding-like base of mayonnaise or salad dressing is frequently used in frozen salads, too.

Frozen salads are usually made in refrigerator freezing trays or loaf pans. Since these salads are usually very firm when removed from the freezer, let the salad set at room temperature a few minutes before cutting it into slices or squares. A bed of greens makes an attractive background for frozen salad.

Frosty Salad Loaf

1 8-ounce package cream cheese
1 cup dairy sour cream
1/4 cup sugar
1/4 teaspoon salt
1 1/2 cups pitted, halved fresh dark
   sweet cherries
1 16-ounce can apricot halves,
   drained and sliced
1 8 3/4-ounce can crushed pineapple,
   drained
2 cups miniature marshmallows
   Few drops red food coloring
   Salad greens
   Pitted cherries
   Peach slices

Let cream cheese stand at room temperature to soften. Then, beat fluffy. Stir in sour cream, sugar, and salt, then fruits and marshmallows. Add few drops red food coloring to tint pale pink. Pour into an 8 1/2x4 1/2x2 5/8-inch loaf pan. Freeze about 6 hours or overnight.

To serve let stand out a few minutes, then remove from container, slice, and place on crisp salad greens. Trim with pitted cherries and peach slices. Makes 8 servings.

Frozen Fruit Slices

2 3-ounce packages cream cheese,
   softened
1 cup mayonnaise or salad dressing
1 30-ounce can fruit cocktail,
   well drained
1/2 cup maraschino cherries, well
   drained and quartered
2 1/2 cups miniature marshmallows
1 cup whipping cream
   Few drops red food coloring *or*
   maraschino cherry juice

In mixing bowl blend together cream cheese and mayonnaise. Stir in fruit cocktail, cherries, and marshmallows. Whip whipping cream; fold into fruit mixture. Tint with food coloring or cherry juice, if desired.

Pour into two 1-quart round ice cream containers or refrigerator-freezer trays. Freeze firm, about 6 hours or overnight. To serve, let stand out a few minutes, then remove from containers; slice. Serves 10 to 12.

Frosty Fruit Molds

1 8-ounce package cream cheese,
   softened
1/4 cup mayonnaise or salad dressing
1/4 cup sifted confectioners' sugar
2 tablespoons lemon juice
1/2 teaspoon vanilla
1 10-ounce package frozen blueberries, thawed and drained
1 10-ounce package frozen peaches,
   thawed, drained, and cut up
1 8 3/4-ounce can pineapple tidbits,
   drained
1 cup miniature marshmallows
1 cup whipping cream

Combine cream cheese, mayonnaise, confectioners' sugar, lemon juice, and vanilla; beat smooth. Fold in fruits and marshmallows. Whip cream; fold into fruit mixture. Turn into 12 individual molds or one 6 1/2-cup mold; freeze.

Before serving, allow salads to stand at room temperature, 10 minutes for individual molds and 20 minutes for 6 1/2-cup mold. Serves 12.

Spicy Peach Freeze

1 29-ounce can peach slices
1/2 of one 6-ounce can frozen orange
   juice concentrate, thawed
4 inches stick cinnamon
5 whole cloves
2 3-ounce packages cream cheese,
   softened
3 tablespoons mayonnaise
1 cup whipping cream

Drain peaches, reserving syrup. Chop peaches; set aside. In small saucepan combine reserved syrup, orange juice concentrate, cinnamon, and cloves; bring to boiling. Reduce heat; simmer, uncovered, for 5 minutes. Remove from heat; cool. Remove spices and discard.

Beat cream cheese with mayonnaise; gradually stir in juice mixture. Add peaches; mix well. Whip cream; fold into fruit mixture. Line 9x9x2-inch baking pan with foil; turn salad into pan. Cover tightly; freeze.

Before serving, lift frozen salad and foil from pan; let stand at room temperature 10 minutes. Remove foil. Cut into pieces; serve on lettuce, if desired. Serves 8 to 10.